DESIGNERS' HANDBOOK OF T-SHIRT PROMOTIONS

Manufactured in
Singapore.

Designers' Handbook of
T-Shirt Promotions
Library of Congress
Catalog Card Number
92-081124
ISBN 1-883915-04-X

RC Publications
**President and
Publisher:**
Howard Cadel
**Vice President and
Editor:**
Martin Fox
Creative Director:
Andrew Kner
Project Manager:
Katherine Nelson
Associate Art Director:
Michele L. Trombley
**Administrative
Assistant:**
Nancy Silver

£23.98
741.6

WITHDRAWN

ESIGNERS' HANDBOOK OF T-SHIRT PROMOTIONS
NNING DESIGNS FROM PRINT MAGAZINE'S NATIONAL DESIGN COMPETITION

Writer/Editor
Pamela A. Ivinski

Art Director
Andrew Kner

Project Manager
Katherine Nelson

Associate Art Director
Michele L. Trombley

Published by
RC Publications, Inc.
New York, NY

CONTENTS

What's more comfortable than a T-shirt? We put them on when we want to step outside our workaday selves, kick back, and relax—even if relaxing means running ten miles or scaling a wall of rock. T-shirts are like pajamas, only we're not embarrassed to be seen wearing them in public. To the contrary, we wear them because we want to be noticed, because we want to be recognized immediately for who we are. Lacrosse player. Member of a church. Mickey Mouse fan. Country music lover. Participant in an AIDS walk. Graphic artist. The *Designers' Handbook of T-Shirt Promotions* features T-shirts making these statements, and many more.

While many T-shirt promotions involve serious issues, designers recognize that levity is an effective way of getting a message across, and the casual nature of the T-shirt medium lends itself to humorous treatment. When asked about the main problem in creating T-shirt promotions of all sorts, designer after designer told us, "Creating something fun, something that people will wear." A tee that never gets taken out of a drawer is a waste of cotton. A tee that's well-loved still gets worn, even after holes begin to appear.

Designers' Handbook of T-Shirt Promotions, from *PRINT* magazine's new *Handbook* series, explains how designers create the tees that bring in business, promote charitable causes, and express personal achievements and beliefs—the T-shirts that get worn. The best T-shirt promotions from *PRINT*'s 1995 and 1996 Regional Design Annuals are reproduced here in large-size visuals, accompanied, when appropriate, by collateral materials such as brochures and mailers. A short commentary for each promotion provides information such as intended audience, source of imagery, choice of illustrator, printing restrictions, type of software used, budget, and size of print run.

The shirts are divided into seven categories according to type of client: Arts & Engineering, Companies & Services, Restaurants & Food, Sports, Religion & Charity, Museums & Attractions, and Retail. Each category is further divided into two sub-categories, to allow for more specific comparison within each group. Short essays introducing the categories and sub-categories provide additional information, such as trends and innovations.

More than other assignments, T-shirt promotions are labors of love. They provide designers with a chance to let loose, push the boundaries, have some fun. And when everything comes together and the result is a great T-shirt, the designer is rewarded with a uniquely public tribute—after all, no one parades around in an annual report. With this *Designers' Handbook of T-Shirt Promotions*, *PRINT* is pleased to offer you the opportunity to learn from—and enjoy—some of the best.—*Pamela A. Ivinski*

T-shirts are fun; there's no questioning that fact. Many T-shirts promoting design firms and design and arts organizations and events are funny as well as fun. Of the 14 promotions featured in this section, only Pennebaker Design's tenth anniversary shirt (p. 12) takes a completely serious approach, in keeping with the achievement of a significant business milestone.

The rest of the T-shirt promotions in this section utilize visual and verbal puns, whimsical figures, even good old dirty jokes to draw attention to the art of design. Clive Cochran's competition-winning "Official Graphic Arts Society T-shirt Design" (p. 28) takes a self-reflexive approach: The type solution offers helpful user instructions such as "This side toward front" and "Periodic laundering recommended. Remove before washing." A number of other tees employ front-to-back puns, and two of these make homophonic reference to the firm's name. Dreier Design's logo, seen on the back of three self-promo shirts (pp. 18-19), plays on the similar sounds of (Kyle) Dreier and a (clothes) dryer. The image of the Dreier dryer is manipulated with repeats, colors, and decorative patterns for front-of-the-shirt designs. For Austin, Texas, firm Tocquigny Advertising & Design, the rhyming puns on three T-shirts (pp. 20-23) serve to teach a valuable lesson: how to pronounce a potentially difficult name. Big Bang Idea Engineering gives visual form to a name that implies high-impact design: The building that serves as the company logo, seen on the front of the shirt (p. 24) explodes on the back (p. 25). The bawdy line on the front of Frank E.E. Grubich's tee (p. 9) is guaranteed to cause double-takes. While the back (p. 8) "explains" the joke—the name of Grubich's firm is Laughing Dog Creative—the initial effect is not diminished.

An animal motif is evident on a number of other tees in this section. EvansGroup designer Marian McDevitt depicted a clown doing a handstand on a leopard for a tee distributed to the agency's employees to encourage attendance at a summer party (p. 10). Christopher Mayes invented an oceanful of musical sea creatures for a shirt commemorating CHP & Associates' participation in the American Institute of Architects' 1994 Steelcase competition (p. 29), which requires the "engineering" of sand castles. Calzone & Associates, too, mixed the actual with the fanciful in a "Mardi Gras Mayhem" promotion for the Louisiana Film Commission (pp. 30-32). A alligator decorated with fairy tale scenes and a banner-waving elf evoke the singular nature of Louisiana's culture and landscape. A squirrel, a bunny, a dog, and a cat with a mouse standing between its ears join the skiing, skating, and sledding humans on Lehner & Whyte's 1995 winter promotion T-shirt (p. 13), which speaks to the joyousness of the holiday season in a non-sectarian way.

Other design firms and organizations turn to signature figures to represent themselves. "Dr. Fish," the "mad" scientist on a shirt by Next Year's News (p. 11) started life as an image printed on packing tissue. His popularity led to the establishment of Fishsandwych, a T-shirt company spin-off of Next Year's News. "Pencil-head," the brainchild of Susan Gros and Bill Koeb, represents the illustrators, designers, and photographers who comprise the San Francisco "Lonely Arts Club" (pp. 26-27). John Sayles's many hand-drawn figures decorate a number of T-shirts celebrating the unique qualities of Sayles Graphic Design's "One of a Kind," "Cutting Edge," and "Tip Top" efforts, and nine years in the business as well (pp. 14-17).

In past PRINT books featuring T-shirt designs, text-based ad agency promotions were legion. In this book, the balance tips in favor of graphic design firms, who tend to represent themselves with images rather than words. Verbal play is not absent, however. Tocquigny Advertising & Design's tees (pp. 20-22) rhyme the firm's name with, fun objects (bikini, zucchini, martini). Dreier Design's logo also exploits a rhyming pun and the Dreier dryer appears on a series of three shirts (pp. 18-19), transformed into decorative designs with a retro feel. Big Bang Idea Engineering's logo, an art deco building, is retro, too. For a self-promo tee (pp. 24-25), the agency's edifice is subjected to a visual "big bang," exploded on the back of the shirt. Laughing Dog Creative's shirt (this spread) exploits a number of visual/verbal puns on its

name, ranging from the intellectual to the salacious.

Two shirts shown in this section, denoting anniversaries, rely more on text than image. For its 10th year, Pennebaker Design (p. 12) created a restrained T-shirt that forms the zero in the number 10 from a spiral of words announcing the reason for celebration. John Sayles Design's ninth anniversary shirt (p. 16) employs text clippings as design elements, in keeping with that firm's penchant for public relations. In contrast, a Lehner & Whyte holiday shirt (p. 13) and a tee for an EvansGroup holiday party (p. 10) eschew text in favor of charming scenes packed with activity, and Next Year's News promotes "pure visual energy" to medical industry and associations clients with an image suggestive of a "mad scientist" knocked out of his socks (p. 11).

Design Firm:
Laughing Dog Creative,
Inc., Chicago, IL
Art Director:
Frank E.E. Grubich
Designers:
Frank E.E. Grubich,
Tim Meyer

LAUGHING DOG CREATIVE, INC.

Frank E.E. Grubich is succinct when explaining the intended effect of Laughing Dog Creative's self-promotion T-shirt: "To be funny," he says. On the back of the shirt, hand-drawn art featuring a dog collar and leash, a dog house, a hot-doggy dog, and a very large bone inscribed with a designer's pun, "There's no Haus like Bow Haus," carries out the Laughing Dog theme. As for unusual or special use of software, Grubich reports that he had a problem with a wobbly leveling table, but "three diskettes did the job!" And regarding any other interesting or unusual aspects of the T-shirt's production, Grubich says of the ribald pun on its front, "My mother didn't get the joke."

EvansGroup, a Salt Lake City agency involved in advertising, direct marketing, and public relations, needed a T-shirt to raise enthusiasm among employees for a summer party that had generally suffered from poor attendance. Designer Marian McDevitt sought to communicate whimsy and fun through a brightly-colored illustration of a circus theme. Paper cut-outs were scanned into a Mac for final production art, and a good printing deal was struck with a silkscreen company seeking EvansGroup business. Though the design was not unanimously satisfactory to a party committee, some of whom objected to the clown ("too young") and the leopard ("should be a horse"), McDevitt's image was approved. Ultimately, the T-shirt was well-liked by EvansGroup employees, in spite of the fact, says McDevitt, that "advertising people are picky."

Design Firm:
EvansGroup,
Salt Lake City, UT
Designer:
Marian McDevitt
Production:
Brian Jones

When contacting medical industry and associations clients after distributing their 1994 "Pure Visual Energy" promo, designers at Next Year's News were surprised to find its printed packing tissue tacked up like a poster on many clients' walls. In response to the unexpected popularity of this design, the image was reworked and used for the NYN 1995 summer T-shirt self-promotion. This, in turn, led to the formation of a T-shirt company, called Fishsandwych. (The Fishsandwych logo appears on the back of the shirt.) The depiction of "Dr. Fish," a "mad" (yet politically correct) scientist with red-target eyeglasses (and a nuclear symbol close by) on the front of the tee suggests the dynamic impact of Next Year's News' design, while at the same time standing alone as an amusing image. The shirt was printed in 2-color using an Antec 6-color textile press.

NEXT YEAR'S NEWS, INC.

Design Firm:
Next Year's News, Inc.,
Toledo, OH
Art Director:
Dwight Ashley
Designer/Illustrator:
Chris Hoffman

Pennebaker Design's tenth anniversary T-shirt served both as a souvenir for attendees at the firm's 1995 celebratory party and as a promotion given to current and potential clients. Designer Haesun Kim Lerch achieved a crisp look with three colors printed on black. The typographic spiral representing a zero also emphasizes the solidity of the digit at left, suggesting that Pennebaker Design is "number one" and "one-of-a-kind."

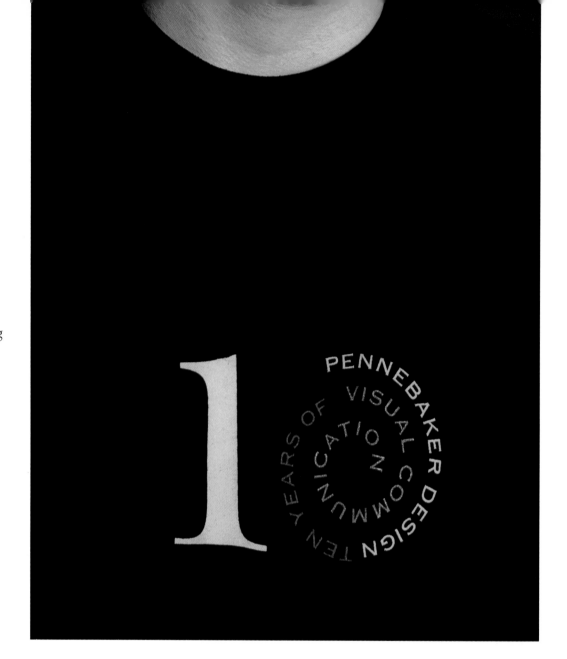

Design Firm:
Pennebaker Design,
Houston, Texas
Art Director/Designer/Illustrator:
Haesun Kim Lerch

Clients of Lehner & Whyte have come to expect amusing and high-quality holiday self-promotions from the Montclair, New Jersey, design firm. They weren't disappointed with 1995's offering, a T-shirt on the theme of outdoor winter fun. Because Lehner & Whyte desired a non-sectarian image, holiday colors here are unusual but effective: Black-silhouetted kids, adults, and animals frolic against a lilac-and-white background. The art was created in Adobe Illustrator. Two-color printing kept costs down; the combined budget for printing and postage was $2500.

LEHNER & WHYTE, INC.

Design Firm:
Lehner & Whyte, Inc.,
Montclair, NJ
**Art Directors/
Designers/Illustrators:**
Donna Lehner,
Hugh Whyte

John Sayles's design style is instantly recognizable to anyone who has seen his work. Four self-promotion T-shirts intended as thank-you gifts for Sayles Graphic Design's loyal clients and vendors exploit his signature look while also making reference to the fact that it is created without the use of computers. One shirt, emblazoned with the boast "One of a Kind Design" (this page), emphasizes that claim with the repeated motif of a "number one" gesture performed by a crowned figure, He carries a gift—presumably that of award-winning design. Another figure holds an immense X-acto knife to embody hand-rendered yet "Cutting Edge Design" (opposite page). "Tip Top Design" (p. 17) is represented by a top-hatted figure who waves a pencil like a successful businessman might hold a celebratory cigar. The pencil also appears with a triangle and top hat on the shirt's sleeve. The fourth shirt (p. 16) denotes that Sayles's firm had racked up nine years of great design by 1995. Clippings from articles praising the company serve as design elements, along with a quote from Sayles set in large type, again stressing his feelings about the computer and design.

Design Firm:
Sayles Graphic Design,
Des Moines, Iowa
**Art Director/Designer/
Illustrator:**
John Sayles

Dreier Design's logo plays on the homophony between principal Kyle Dreier's surname and the word for a common household appliance. The logo employs a stylized drawing of a clothes dryer to give the pun visual form. The three self-promotion T-shirts shown here, created "almost for self-gratification," according to the firm, push the '50s-ish optimism of the original logo to a giddy extreme. Embellished with repeats and punchy colors, the designs become almost abstract and decorative, though the Dreier dryer remains recognizable. Three versions were created "just for fun," so that different employees within the same client companies could enjoy some variety. No unusual production techniques were employed; the printing budget totaled $1000.

Design Firm:
Dreier Design, Dallas, TX
Designers:
Kyle D. Dreier,
Deanna Schneider

TOCQUIGNY ADVERTISING & DESIGN

How to pronounce the name of this Austin firm—Tocquigny Advertising & Design—can be something of a mystery, at least until you see one of these clever T-shirts. Designer Lori Walls succeeded in teaching an unforgettable lesson while creating an appealing summer self-promotion with these three shirts on the theme of "Sounds like . . .," which appears on the back of each tee. Walls's illustrations of a polka-dotted bikini (opposite page), a refreshing martini (p. 22), and the ubiquitous late-summer zucchini (p. 23), rendered in cartoonish style, get the message across with a minimum of fuss.

[sounds like]

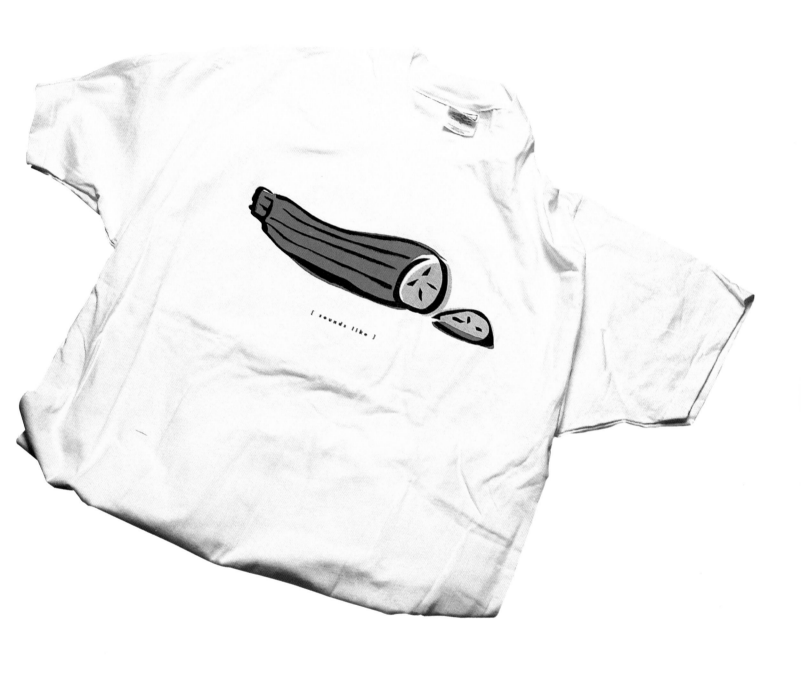

[sounds like]

Design Firm:
Tocquigny Advertising
& Design,
Austin, TX
Designer/Illustrator:
Lori Walls

Big Bang Idea Engineering, a full-service advertising agency, opened its doors in May 1995. The concept for this self-promotion T-shirt derives from the company's corporate identity. Big Bang's creative directors began by selecting a type style to convey intelligence and business sense because, despite the flashy name, they consider the agency to be "a buttoned-up business." Inspired by an actual building in Seattle that almost became home to the agency, they searched public domain art and architectural renderings, discovering a drawing of an art deco building that embodied Big Bang's idea of modern corporate culture. Once they had the symbol of the building, which serves as both their logo and the design on the front of the shirt, they decided to "blow it up" for the "reveal" on the back of the tee. This, they report, required some illustrative finesse, accomplished in Adobe Illustrator and Quark XPress. Special care was taken to ensure that the screen inks used on the shirt matched the PMS inks printed on the company's stationery package. Printing cost about $7 per shirt.

BIG BANG IDEA ENGINEERING

WADE KONIAKOWSKY, CREATIVE DIRECTOR
6820 XANA WAY, CARLSBAD, CA 92009
PHONE 619·471·5445 FAX 619·591·4430

Design Firm:
Big Bang Idea Engineering,
Carlsbad, CA
Art Director/Illustrator:
Wade Koniakowsky
Copywriter:
Robert Bagot
Creative Directors:
Wade Koniakowsky,
Robert Bagot

The T-shirts in this section promote design, engineering, and
arts organizations and related
events. The imagery ranges
from busy and joyous to
restrained and poignant, but
all with a touch of whimsy.
Designs for CHP & Associates,
Consulting Engineers, and the
Louisiana Film Commission
depict creatures great and
small, actual and mythical, in
jam-packed tableaux.
Christopher Mayes's "Sand
Dudes," the shirt promoting
CHP's participation in the
American Institute of
Architects Steelcase competition (p. 29), features psychedel-
ic sea animals far more colorful
than anything found even in
the most gorgeous real-life reef.
Though rendered in black-and-
white, the cats, mice, brownies,
and man-in-the-moon drawn
by Doug Kennedy of Calzone &
Associates for the Louisiana
Film Commission tees (pp.30-
32) are just as colorful in their
gestures and expressions.

In his competition-winning
design for the official Graphic
Arts Society of El Paso T-shirt
(p. 28), Clive Cochran turned
the problem into the solution,
with a self-referential, text-
based rough for the shirt design
used as the actual design. In
contrast, a simple tee for the
San Francisco "Lonely Arts
Club" (this spread), by Susan
Gross and Bill Koeb, depicts
two icons, a "Pencil-head"
figure and a heart, to capture
the mood of this group of generally solitary art and design
professionals.

Susan Gross and Bill Koeb describe their assignment for the "Lonely Arts Club" as "designing a T-shirt for an opinionated group of illustrators, designers, and photographers who meet in San Francisco on a monthly basis." "Pencil-head" was invented as a simple icon to identify the group. Gross drew the outline for the figure and the heart logo, while Koeb filled them in with a 4-color textured painting. The images were made into iron-ons and applied to the shirts, all on a shoestring budget. The T-shirts were originally meant for used by the "Lonely Arts Club" bowling team only, but their popularity led to club-wide adoption.

THE "LONELY ARTS CLUB"

Design Firm:
Susan Gross
Illustration & Design,
San Francisco, CA
Designers/Illustrators:
Susan Gross, Bill Koeb

GRAPHIC ARTS SOCIETY OF EL PASO

Designer Clive Cochran of Mithoff Advertising won a competition for the official T-shirt of the Graphic Arts Society of El Paso with this amusing design. According to Cochran, "the problem dictated the solution." Thus, he created the design around the problem of creating the design for the official Graphic Arts Society T-shirt. He intended the lettering to look spontaneous, yet retain the formal qualities of design. Indeed, all the shirt's elements were carefully balanced, yet designed to look "not designed." Cochran reports that the lettering was done with india ink and a "very old, much abused brush . . . an old friend" that frequently yields unpredictable results. As for the use of a computer, Cochran says, "the only software used was the designer's brain, which has gotten considerably softer." He donated the design to the Society; printing costs for 60 shirts totaled $510.

Design Firm:
Mithoff Advertising,
El Paso, TX
**Art Director/Designer/
Copywriter:**
Clive Cochran

Christopher Mayes Design created this T-shirt for CHP & Associates, Consulting Engineers, to promote the firm's participation in the American Institute of Architects' 1994 Steelcase competition, which involves building sand castles. Mayes chose to illustrate an ocean-going theme of "Sand Dudes" rather than depicting his own vision of what an engineer's sand castle might look like. His whimsical sea creatures, such as a guitar-strumming octopus and a drumstick-wielding starfish, bring to mind Beatles songs, such as "Yellow Submarine" or "Octopus's Garden." Mayes's hand-drawn art was scanned, streamlined, and colorized in Adobe Illustrator, and printed with a 6-color silkscreen automatic process.

Design Firm:
Christopher Mayes
Design, Houston, TX
Designer/Illustrator:
Christopher Mayes

CHP & ASSOCIATES, CONSULTING ENGINEERS

The Louisiana Film Commission was set up to attract film and video production to the state. Calzone & Associates produced these T-shirts and collateral materials to be distributed at "Mardi Gras Mayhem," a special event held at the House of Blues in Hollywood in conjunction with "Location Expo." The festivity of Mardi Gras and drawings of imaginary "critters" combine with regional imagery such as the alligator to promote the unique charms of Louisiana. The illustrations were drawn by Mojoware, and the T-shirts were handprinted using Plastisol inks. Accompanying materials included an invitation and reply card, state-specific location information, and custom Mardi Gras beads. Through this event and other Calzone & Associates promotional efforts on behalf of the Film Commission, the state of Louisiana has doubled its film and video business, reaching $100-million dollars.

Design Firm:
Calzone & Associates,
Lafayette, LA
Art Director:
Laurie Landry
Illustrator:
Mojoware
Artist:
Doug Kennedy
Production:
John Kennedy
Printing:
Chris Fleming

Take a picture, it lasts longer" reads the headline on one T-shirt in this section. What kinds of pictures appear on shirts promoting companies and services (many of them related to the design industry) in this section? Three shirts make use of iconic figures, three employ images by illustrators known for signature styles, and two display pictures made from type. Only one shirt has a type-only design.

The iconic figure on Jeff Labbé's tee for Kimball Hall Photography (the "Take a picture" shirt mentioned above; p. 36) is that of the photographer himself, represented in an abstracted style, an "inner vision" of the artist. The positive/negative figure in DogStar Design & Illustration's logo for Digital Prepress Services (p. 37) embodies the typical DPS employee: expert, helpful, and swift. Ted Wright's "jackhammer man" (p. 38) possesses similar qualities in an entirely different kind of industry: concrete construction. Working with Solomon Turner Advertising, Wright learned that those who work with concrete consider themselves to be artists no less than a photographer or prepress expert: "artists with a jackhammer."

Illustrator Burton Morris produced a number of "art garments" in his easily-recognizable style (pp. 39-41) to promote the services of Energy Gear, the printed promotional materials company he co-founded with printing pro Jeffry Dunn. Images such as "Big Hitter" (p. 39) demonstrate the engaging nature of his signature look, and a brochure (p. 40) offers successful campaigns such as that for the aperitif Dubonnet (see also the Morris–illustrated Dubonnet T-shirt on p. 112). For a series of three T-shirts, BMC Software hired Christopher Mayes and his high-energy illustration skills (pp. 48-50). Mayes turned ordinary office equipment and computer gear into collage elements, with the *0*'s and *1*'s of binary language providing decorative (and literally) digital punctuation. The resulting images celebrate the software company by transcending actual products. A T-shirt by José Bila Rodríguez of POD for Xerox Corp.'s DDS Division (p. 46) also makes only oblique reference to the final product, in this case the a piece of multipurpose office equipment with a cube shape. The ultimate meaning of the assignment—to create a design incorporating a drawing of a cactus (for the "Cactus Project") and the headline "More than a box"—was somewhat vague even to the designer due to the secret nature of the product (still hush-hush at this book's press time).

The final three designs in this section highlight type treatments. A T-shirt for Type Case prepress services of Fort Worth, Texas (following spread), created by Rishi Seth of Witherspoon Advertising, builds the figure of a cow out of the letters in "Cowtown," a nickname for Fort Worth. Andrea Peterson of SullivanPerkins also employed type in a figurative way for a tee commissioned by public relations firm Meltzer & Martin (pp. 44-45). Peterson used type that mimics chalk marks to commemorate five years "chalked up" in the PR industry. In contrast to this terse statement, Dan De Witt's T-shirt for Yes Computers (pp. 42-43) says something deceptively simple in a deceptively complicated way. What at first appears to be more than an exercise in layered "grunge" type turns out to be a pun on the computer company's name, constructed out of the many ways to say "Yes" without actually saying it.

The T-shirts in this section demonstrate that a bold and simple figural style is favored for the promotion of companies and services to the public—with one notable exception. Energy Gear, a collaboration between an illustrator and a printer, makes use of Burton Morris's vibrant outlines and colors to sell its promotional design services (pp. 39-41). Solomon Turner Advertising also looked to a strong illustrator, Ted Wright, for its "jackhammer man," who represents Coffman Bros. Construction (p. 38). Jeff Labbé, designing for a fellow art client, Kimball Hall Photography, developed a more abstract yet still figural logo with strong lines and shapes (p. 36). DogStar Design exploited the positive/negative qualities of black on white in a figural logo for Digital Prepress Services (p. 37). Black-and-white alone is also used for two T-shirts in this section, one for Type Case prepress services (this spread), the other for Yes Computers, an Apple Macintosh dealer (pp. 42-43). Witherspoon Advertising promotes Fort Worth's Type Case with a cow formed from the letters in "Cowtown," the city's "affectionate" nickname. Type, form, and headline combine to elucidate each other. Dann De Witt of De Witt Anthony took the opposite approach with his shirt for young, hip customers of Yes Computers (pp. 42-43). A hodgepodge of words and phrases in grunge lettering means something ("Yes") without directly saying it, as does his design.

It was important to Type Case, a Fort Worth, Texas, prepress service, that their promotional tee avoid reading like an overt advertisement. Witherspoon Advertising responded with a type solution, giving Fort Worth's nickname, "Cowtown," visual form through lettering, along with the punning headline, "Cowtown is my type of place." On the back is the company logo, reading—and rhyming with the phrase on the front—Type Case. The wordform was created in Adobe Illustrator. The design was donated and the printing budge was $300, for two hits of white on a black shirt.

Design Firm:
Witherspoon Advertising, Fort Worth, TX
Art Director/Designer/ Illustrator/Copywriter:
Rishi Seth
Creative Director:
Debra Morrow

Kimball Hall Photography looked to Jeff Labbé Design Co. for a T-shirt to be used to thank valued clients. The shirt also needed to promote a new identity for Kimball Hall. The front of the tee displays a stylized line drawing of a tripod, in black. The line drawing style is carried over to the back of the shirt, where blocks of color were added to an "inner vision" or abstract portrait of the photographer behind the camera. The company name and phone number are integrated into the "portrait" as well. The design was created in Adobe Illustrator for $3000; printing of the shirts, which involved custom mixing of two PMS colors for the image on the back, cost $4 each.

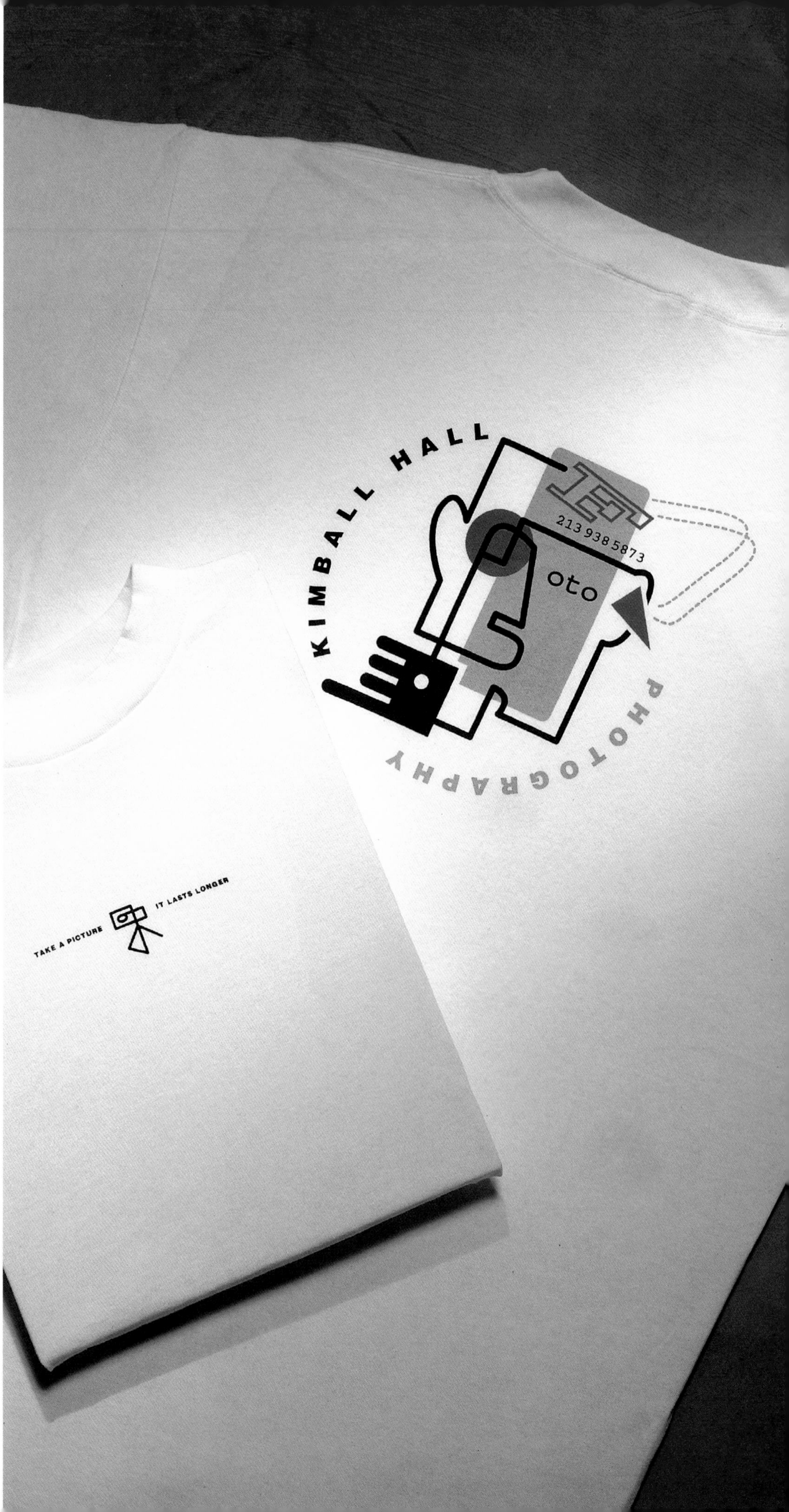

Design Firm:
Jeff Labbé Design Co.,
San Francisco, CA
Art Director/Designer:
Jeff Labbé

Designer Rodney Davidson of DogStar Design & Illustration traded his talents for production provided by Digital Prepress Services (DPS). The design seen on this T-shirt also serves as the service bureau's corporate identity. Because Davidson admires the high standards, work ethic, and "clients first" attitude of DPS, he was inspired to capture these qualities in a logo. He also wanted something that would look like a screen icon and reflect technological expertise; something simple but interesting. The resulting positive/negative black-and-white design presents a DPS employee handing pages or proofs over the counter to a customer. A spiky black pattern shadowing the top page also suggests fast-moving service. The front of the shirt sports a small version of the logo, with "Digital Prepress Services" spelled out at right. Approximately 200 T-shirts were printed for $5 each.

Design Firm:
DogStar Design &
Illustration,
Birmingham, Alabama
Designer/Illustrator:
Rodney Davidson

COFFMAN BROS. INC.

If you need to solve a major construction problem or to alleviate a dangerous structural situation in the St. Louis area, you call Coffman Bros. Construction. The company commissioned this T-shirt as a promotion for engineers and construction workers in the concrete industry. The assignment for the designers at Solomon Turner Advertising: Create a bold, exciting graphic that brings pride and distinction to a hardworking and dirty profession. From discussions with the client, Solomon Turner learned that concrete workers consider themselves to be "artists with a jackhammer." A "jackhammer man," then, had to be created. Missouri illustrator Ted Wright was called in to come up with an instantly recognizable image. The purpose of his graphic, says Wright, is to tell you that, "when these guys pull up in their trucks, they are there to solve your structural problem—and save your ass." Adobe Illustrator was used for color separations; the shirts were printed in 9-color.

Design Firm:
Solomon Turner
Advertising,
Hillsboro, MO
Art Directors:
Shelley Solomon,
John Coffman
Designer/Illustrator:
Ted Wright

What is Energy Gear? According to its brochure, "T-shirts, bags, towels, water bottles; any promotional material that needs to generate a lot of interest." Energy Gear is also a company that produces printed promotional materials, a collaboration between illustrator Burton Morris and printing pro Jeffry Dunn. Morris designed the Energy Gear promotional booklet to attract clients, featuring, of course, T-shirts. Mailings of shirts sporting his arty and kinetic designs such as "Big Hitter" or a sunglasses-wearing armadillo have brought in a good deal of business. Even better, the "Big Hitter" tee was worn by one of the characters in an episode of the sitcom *Friends*. The "Big Hitter" shirt was generated in Corel 6 and printed with Plastisol inks. The printing budget for 250 shirts was $1200.

Design Firm:
Burton Morris
Illustration, Pittsburgh, PA
Designer/Illustrator:
Burton Morris

YES COMPUTERS

Yes Computers sells, services, and supports Apple Macintosh computers and accessories. Dann De Witt of De Witt Anthony designed this T-shirt with the company's cool, hip, and loyal customer following in mind. Along with the requisite Apple logo (in solid red), the front of the shirt presents a mess of type, à la *Ray Gun* magazine, that at first appears illegible. Upon closer examination—and the intention of the shirt is to promote closer examination—various words and phrases can be made out: OK, for sure, yeah, definitely, oui, no problemo, of course, uh huh, you bet. All ways to say "Yes" without actually saying it. The back of the shirt provides the punchline: the Yes Computers logo. De Witt Anthony produced the shirt in exchange for computer support and consulting.

Design Firm:
De Witt Anthony, Inc.,
Northampton, MA
**Creative Director/
Designer:**
Dann De Witt

The three shirts in this section, intended for internal distribution within companies, represent different responses to corporate culture. The essence of public relations is getting the message across. Thus, a tee by SullivanPerkins commemorating the fifth anniversary of the PR firm Meltzer & Martin (this spread) makes its point in terse fashion. The letters "MM" crossed with a slash effectively summarize the five years "chalked up" by the company. In contrast to this restrained design, shirts for BMC Software and Xerox Corp. attempt to inject a little anarchic humor into the usually sober information industries. POD's design for Xerox's Cactus Project (pp. 46-47) has the quality of an in-joke, with its spiky plant and headline, "More than a box." Three tees for BMC software (pp. 48-50) take advantage of Christopher Mayes's gentle surrealism. Mayes transforms the mundane stuff of the software industry—floppy disks, monitors, screen icons, even binary language—into joyful compositions celebrating the company, attendance at a music and comedy performance held during a technical conference, and even a "Software Patrol."

SullivanPerkins designer Andrea Peterson developed this wittily simple T-shirt to commemorate the fifth anniversary of public relations firm Meltzer & Martin. For the front of the shirt, intended as a gift for company employees, the initials "MM" are written as if in chalk and crossed with a slash, to picture five years in business. On the back, the words "Chalk Up Another Year For Meltzer & Martin" are dropped out of a "chalk mark" drawn across the shirt at shoulder level. The design was created by SullivanPerkins in trade for Meltzer & Martin PR services.

MELTZER & MARTIN

Design Firm:
SullivanPerkins,
Dallas, TX
Art Director/Designer:
Andrea Peterson

Xerox Corp. hired POD to develop a T-shirt, stationery, and mailing labels for its DDS division. The goal was to build camaraderie and team spirit around a product launch known as the Cactus Project. The only requirement was to include a rendering of a cactus and the tag line "More than a box," to symbolize that the product in development—a multipurpose piece of office equipment in the shape of a cube —would offer more than meets the eye. Designer/ illustrator José Bila Rodríguez gave a warm and friendly face to a very complex technology while also retaining a hip and youthful edge. He drew the main image with pen and ink on bond paper, adding green, yellow, and purple to the printed design with a stipple effect.

Design Firm:
POD, Coral Gables, FL
Art Director:
Elizabeth Ingebretsen
Illustrator:
José Bila Rodríguez

Christopher Mayes Design illustrated these three T-shirts for BMC Software with the intention of promoting the company in a new, refreshing way. All three designs integrate the *0* and *1* of binary language, various tools of the computer trade, and office supplies into upbeat, decorative constructions. Scalloped and jagged edges and flourishes resembling crowns increase the vibrancy of bright colors set off with black. The first shirt (this page), reading simply "BMC Software," is the most "orderly" of the three, perhaps because it was distributed to clients as well as employees. Boxes containing computer-related equipment are contained within a larger box punctuated with *0*'s and *1*'s. A second shirt (next page), commemorating a performance by comedian Paula Poundstone and musical group Tower of Power at the DB2 technical conference, clothes Poundstone in binary language and surrounds her with musical instruments. On the front of the shirt, an emblem in the shape of a ticket furthers the performance motif. A third shirt (p. 50), promoting BMC's "Software Patrol," makes use of a black-and-white cowhide pattern in addition to the energetic collage of computer and office accessories.

Design Firm:
Christopher Mayes
Design, Houston, TX
Designer/Illustrator:
Christopher Mayes

The food-related T-shirt promotions in this section rely mainly upon two types of appeal: upscale and/or surreal. Except for Dana Willett's tees for Kilwin's Chocolate and Ice Cream Shops of Blowing Rock, North Carolina (following spread), almost overwhelming with their luscious cones, little food-as-food is seen on these shirts. When food appears, it is likely to be depicted with strange characters or has come to life as a character in itself.

Of those T-shirts with an upscale appeal, two go the nostalgic route. José Bila Rodríguez's Cubist still life, for a shirt repositioning Le Chic French Bakery from a provider of wholesale baked goods to the owner of a coffee shop and bakery (p. 62), rejects the recent Starbucks model in favor of a more traditional, romantic example: the Parisian pâtisserie. To promote Chicago's Foodlife food stands (definitely not your ordinary mall food court, according to owner Lettuce Entertain You), Sharon Box of Adrienne Weiss Corporation drew a sketchily rendered figure of a woman returning from market, fresh produce filling her basket (p. 55). A large sunhat and seagulls in the background evoke the milieu of summer vacations, when fruits and vegetables are absolutely fresh and the days are less hurried. A T-shirt for Truffles Café & Catering (p. 54), on the other hand, highlights a specific venue for the company, to the complete exclusion of any reference to food (except for the name "Truffles"). The 2-color design emphasizes the Fraze Pavilion experience as a whole—music by the Dayton Philharmonic performed in an outdoor theater-in-the-round, with comestibles provided by Truffles.

The designs on Christopher Pyle's T-shirts for Puccini's Pizza & Pasta Restaurants (following spread) were first created to adorn the walls of the franchise's restaurants. But instead of promoting a restrained vision such as that seen on the Truffles shirt, Pyle's images present over-the-top eating experiences; a little mysterious, and very humorous. Cap Pannell's figures for Bruegger's Bagel Bakery, such as "Sarge" (p. 60), patterned after the Texas A&M mascot, lean more in the direction of humorous, as do his posters for the bakery company (p. 61), which invoke historical personages such as Leonardo da Vinci and Sigmund Freud for a bit of fun. Ward Schumaker's strolling slice of bread (pp. 58-59), the charming figure representing New York City's Columbus Bakery, effectively combines the upscale and the surreal. Somewhat formal in his hat, he seems quite determined to get home, his own loaf of bread tucked under his arm.

Kilwin's Chocolate and Ice Cream Shops of Blowing Rock, North Carolina, are famous for their elaborately named signature flavors, such as Mackinac Island Fudge and Traverse City Cherry. Advertising Design Systems' assignment for a Kilwin's souvenir tee (p. 56) involved displaying the flavors exclusive to the franchise. The result is a shirt that revels in the specific products of this particular company. In contrast, T-shirts for the other three restaurants and food vendors represented in this section lean in the direction of ambiance rather than product. The Foodlife food stands, in an upscale Chicago shopping center, offer environmentally-aware freshness and friendliness. Adrienne Weiss Corporation's T-shirt for Foodlife (p. 55) depicts not a mall scene but rather a freely-rendered woman carrying a basket of produce, in keeping with the Foodlife market philosophy. Graphica's shirt for Truffles Cafe & Catering (p. 54) promotes one particular venue for the company's services: an outdoor theater where the Dayton Philharmonic's summer concerts are played. The tee emphasizes atmosphere (moon, stars, musical notes) over the actual food product. Chris Pyle's T-shirt designs for Puccini's Pizza & Pasta Restaurants (this spread), derived from artworks he created originally to decorate their walls, make reference to the franchise's signature foods, but in an appealing surrealistic fashion.

Indianapolis illustrator Chris Pyle was commissioned originally to create artworks to decorate the walls of three Puccini's Pizza & Pasta Restaurants. The art proved so popular that the restaurants decided to sell T-shirts derived from two of the wall pieces, which carry out a motif of "Smiling Teeth." Each shirt features one of the restaurants' signature dishes: A mysterious, hatted man holds a pizza aloft in one; the hair of a young woman is wrapped, spaghetti-style, around the tines of a fork on the other. A simple, inexpensive printing process, Canon dry transfer, kept costs down for this very limited run. As for the source of his surrealistic visions, Pyle says, "I made all the images up out of my own wittle head."

Design Firm:
Chris Pyle Illustration,
Indianapolis, IN
**Art Director/Designer/
Illustrator:**
Chris Pyle

Graphica designed this T-shirt to promote the catering services of Truffles at one particular venue: the Fraze Pavilion, an intimate, outdoor theater-in-the-round that serves as the home for summer concerts by the Dayton Philharmonic.

A stylized rendering of the pavilion is set against a night sky glowing with moon, stars, musical notes, and a burst of light, to epitomize the Fraze experience for a young, upscale audience. The 2-color printing budget was $2400; the design, $500.

Design Firm:
Graphica,
Miamisburg, OH
Art Director:
Nick Stamas
Designer/Illustrator:
Melissa Bocko Furrey
Production:
Kathy Heming

According to Lettuce Entertain You, a themed restaurant company, Foodlife is not an ordinary food court—it is "a celebration of life and food." Adrienne Weiss Corporation was commissioned to develop an overall identity and marketing/design strategy for this unpretentious group of hip, friendly food stands in a market environment, located in an upscale shopping center in the heart of Chicago. A hangtag proclaims, "Foodlife is environ*mental* . . . Be kind. Eat true. It's now." Sharon Box's illustration and lettering are meant to appear spontaneous and welcoming, in accordance with the Foodlife philosophy. The figure carrying her basket reinforces the idea of freshness and the ambiance of a small town or Old World farmer's market. The shirt is printed in 5-color silkscreen.

Design Firm:
Adrienne Weiss
Corporation,
Los Angeles, CA
**Art Director/Designer/
Illustrator:**
Sharon Box

Kilwin's Chocolate and Ice Cream Shops of Blowing Rock, North Carolina, are famous for their exclusive ice cream flavors, which include Mackinac Island Fudge, Peach Amaretto, Blue Moon, and Traverse City Cherry. Advertising Design Systems created these T-shirts for sale to tourists. Kilwin's signature flavors are displayed and identified on the adult-size shirt (opposite page). Kids, presumably, are less concerned with original flavors than great taste, and the child-sized shirt (this page) simply illustrates every kid's dream cone. Both tees are emblazoned on the back with the slogan, "Life is uncertain . . . eat your dessert first." The illustrations were hand-rendered by Dana Willett.

Design Firm:
Advertising Design Systems, Boone, NC
Art Director/Designer/Illustrator:
Dana Willett

As copycat coffee shops pop up all over the U.S., there is new attention being paid to the foodstuffs that for a time took second place to skinny double caramel mocha whatevers. Bakeries are emerging as an important design client, as the three shirts in this section attest. Le Chic French Bakery, perhaps in response to all the repetitive Seattle- and Starbucks-type imagery now crowding our cities, looked to POD for an updated version of the romantic French café. The resulting T-shirt (p. 62) combines a reference to Cubism with the traditional colors of the French flag. The remaining two designs employ characters to set their baked goods apart. When World Studio hired illustrator Ward Schumaker to develop a logo for New York City's Columbus Bakery, Schumaker and art director Mark Randall agreed that a charming slice of bread, apparently returning from a bakery himself, would best serve to draw customers (this spread). Cap Pannell had already created and used the Bruegger's Bagel Bakery baker figures for a series of promotions. Inventing a new character for T-shirts to be sold at a bakery just opened near the Texas A&M campus simply meant adding to this creative cast (pp. 60-61).

When Mark Randall of World Studio needed a drawing to be used as a logo for Columbus Bakery of New York City, he called Ward Schumaker of San Francisco. Schumaker says, "I'm always trying to produce non-hip, non-elitist illustration." This strolling slice of bread, baguette tucked under his arm, shows that the illustrator has again succeeded. The bread man appears on the front of the shirt; the back says simply, "Columbus Bakery." The charming bread figure is repeated on signage, packaging, coffee cups, and shopping bags, and Randall turned the image into a business card as well, cutting it out in the shape of the slice.

Design Firm:
World Studio,
New York, NY
Art Director:
Mark Randall
Illustrator:
Ward Schumaker

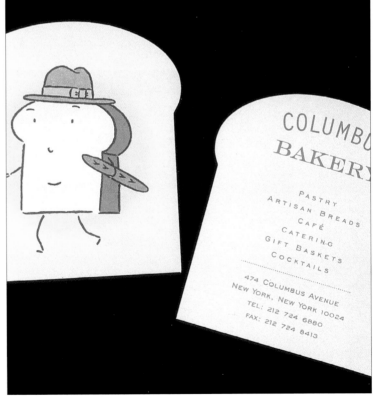

COLUMBU
BAKERY

PASTRY
ARTISAN BREADS
CAFÉ
CATERING
GIFT BASKETS
COCKTAILS

474 COLUMBUS AVENUE
NEW YORK, NEW YORK 10024
TEL: 212 724 6880
FAX: 212 724 8413

Designer/illustrator Cap Pannell of Pannell St. George has had a long-standing relationship with Bruegger's Bagel Bakery, developing promotional material for the franchise as it continues to open new stores throughout the country. For the inauguration of a new bakery near the campus of Texas A&M University in College Station, Bruegger's requested an image to be sold specifically to Aggie students. Pannell responded with this image of Sarge, the A&M mascot, saluting the Bruegger's bakers. The original illustrations were done in pencil on textured paper, scanned into the Macintosh, and colored in Photoshop; the shirts were printed in 4-color process silkscreen.

Design Firm:
Pannell St. George, Dallas, TX
Art Director/Designer/Illustrator:
Cap Pannell

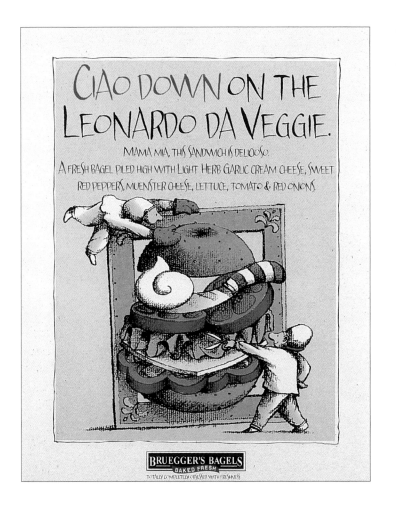

LE CHIC FRENCH BAKERY

Le Chic French Bakery turned to POD when it needed to reposition itself—from a wholesaler of baked goods to a consumer-oriented coffee shop and bakery. Assigned to establish a nostalgic appeal with a contemporary twist, designer/illustrator José Bila Rodríguez combined two different styles for image and type. The café still-life looks to Cubism, with its faceted planes and stippled textures, while the logo and location lines make reference to the red, white, and blue of the French flag. The original image was drawn with pen and ink on bond paper, and two overlays were made, one for each spot color. The main logo and typography were done in Adobe Illustrator.

Design Firm:
POD, Coral Gables, FL
**Art Director/Designer/
Illustrator:**
José Bila Rodríguez

Previous *PRINT* books featuring T-shirt promotions have been dominated by the big guns of sport, particularly Nike and Reebok. The sport-related tees in this volume, in contrast, celebrate lesser-known athletes and events. The Johnson Design Group alludes to the athletic competence of its softball team in its nickname: the Jesters. Norasack Pathammavong's woodcut-like image (p. 67) makes clever use of elements like bats and balls. And lest you think that the jester means this firm is medieval in outlook, a hangtag added to the T-shirt gives the Johnson Design Group Web address, so you can keep up with the most recent scores. The members of Weber Design's volleyball team would probably find it amusing to be considered "athletes" in the same sense as Michael Jordan or Deion Sanders—designer Craig Rouse reports that the "Slammers" aren't exactly volleyball's version of the Chicago Bulls—but in their faux-Bauhaus T-shirts (following spread), they look far better on the court than their rivals, mainly architectural firms.

A number of other tees in this section borrow the streamlined, geometricized forms of modern art movements, to both serious and playful effect. For his Mercury figure for the Barnabas International World Missions Run (p. 74), Scott Johnson says he looked directly to Umberto Boccioni's sculpture, "Unique Forms of Continuity in Space," which depicts an abstracted yet powerful nude figure striding ahead with great determination. Johnson's figure implies movement toward the achievement of Barnabas's missionary work as well as the finish line of the race. Peter Winecke's striding lacrosse player, for a Minneapolis Lacrosse Club T-shirt (p. 66), similarly uses a combination of angles and curves to imply sharp technique and smooth execution on the athletic field. Gordon Studer's building block runners, for the official 1996 *San Francisco Examiner* Bay-to-Breakers marathon tee (p. 73) appear equally swift as the Barnabas Mercury, but they're also cute, and appealing to adults and kids alike.

Ward Schumaker's T-shirts for the 1995 *San Francisco Examiner* Bay-to-Breakers race are designed to appeal to a wide range of participants and spectators, from runners to tourists to kids. His official shirt and poster image (p. 72), commissioned by *San Francisco Examiner* Charities, portrays Mercury, the Roman messenger of the gods, wearing a decidedly un-godlike rubber nose, in tribute to the many runners who participate in the Bay-to-Breakers in costume. Mercury takes a number of different forms for additional T-shirts sold through the Nordstrom department store: a "head-shot" (p. 70), with a cable car for a body (p. 69), and a close-up of his winged foot, about to slip on a banana peel, vaudeville style (p. 71). For a T-shirt aimed at the kid's market (p. 68), Schumaker put Mercury aside in favor of a more child-appropriate image incorporating the tortoise and the hare, traditional symbols of the Bay-to-Breakers.

Logos for sports teams are big business—billion-dollar business. Unfortunately, the mass-market pressures behind the development of new major league logos usually lead to banality or overkill. The three T-shirts displaying sports logos in this section, however, are refreshing and fun, doubtless due, in part, to the fact that the designers are designing for themselves, or for non-traditional sports. Norasack Pathammavong's gloved jester for the Johnson Design Group softball team (p. 67) would well serve a major league franchise: The image embodies fun in combination with eye-catching design. Peter Winecke's positive/negative logo for the Minneapolis Lacrosse Club (p. 66) also provides a lesson for major league clubs: Sports marks can be crisp, fresh, and effective in 2-color, without looking like everyone else's symbol. A T-shirt for Weber Design's volleyball team (this spread) is a little too design in-jokey for widespread use (Bo knows Bauhaus?), but the players who wear it can be assured of "looking good" on the court—no matter their level of athletic skill.

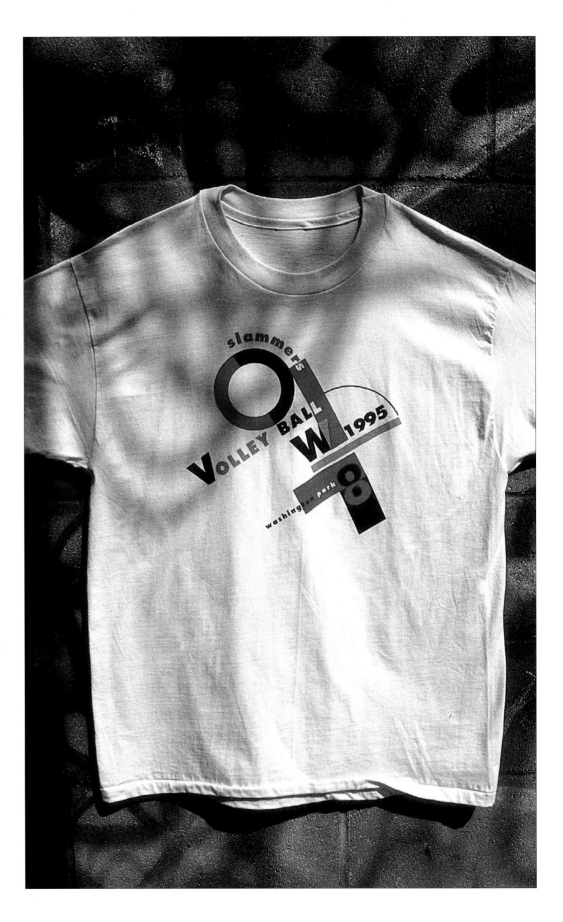

When Weber Design's volleyball team decided to outfit itself, they wanted to produce something that looked "crisp on the court and cool when we're finished," and good on all players. Designers Marty Gregg and Craig Rouse explain, "We wanted to make a statement about precision, so we hitched a ride on Bauhaus style and color, with tongue planted in cheek." While the front of the "Slammers" shirt does make reference to a Bauhaus esthetic with its geometric shapes and use of red and black, the back nods to Dada and to more contemporary design sources such as Nike and Reebok. Various insults prove the team to be adept at verbal as well as volleyball "spikes." Three PMS colors on unbleached shirts led to a total cost of $20 per shirt, plus $5 in "captain's fees," payable to Rouse, for his troubles: He has to attend all league meetings on behalf of the team. Because the league consists mainly of architectural firms, "the meetings are always too long." As an added bonus for team members, the shirts "look even better after a few washes," the designers report.

Design Firm:
Weber Design,
Denver, CO
Designers:
Marty Gregg, Craig
Rouse

MINNEAPOLIS LACROSSE CLUB

Peter Winecke's design for the Minneapolis Lacrosse Club had to work on everything from T-shirts to water bottles and game balls. Because the printing budget was extremely low, Winecke utilized a positive/negative effect, contrasting curves and hard edges in order to create movement and excitement in one color. Winecke's hand-drawn image succeeds in setting apart the Minneapolis Lacrosse Club mark from the usual clichéd sports logo. The positive/negative type treatment and the horizontal lines cut into the first few letters of "Lacrosse" also transform the letter *O* into a streaking lacrosse ball, emblematic of this fast-paced sport.

Design Firm:
Carmichael Lynch,
Minneapolis, MN
Art Director/Designer:
Peter Winecke

Designer Norasack Pathammavong conveys both the fun of sport and the esthetic of Johnson Design Group with this T-shirt for the firm's softball team, the Jesters. Pathammavong added interest to a 2-color design by mimicking a woodcut effect for the image of the softball-playing funnyman, and by employing light tones on a rich green background. With the addition of a hangtag, the shirt also serves as a thank-you gift to clients. The tag explains that the shirt "brought our studio team good luck and a winning season," and adds that up-to-date scores can be found at the firm's Web site, at http://www.jdgdesign.com. Internal design and printing costs totaled $6.50 per shirt; 50 shirts were produced.

Design Firm:
Johnson Design Group, Inc., Falls Church, VA
Art Director/Designer/ Illustrator:
Norasack Pathammavong

JOHNSON DESIGN GROUP

The assignment: Produce a commemorative marathon T-shirt, something runners will be proud to wear as a badge that proclaims, "I survived—all 26 miles"; something that tourists and the less athletically inclined might want to wear, too, as a way of sharing a bit of the glory. The solution, for the three designers featured in this section: Depict . . . a runner. But no ordinary runners, these. Of course, the extraordinary athlete is a natural for the San Francisco Examiner *Bay-to-Breakers* marathon, where anything goes. For the 1995 *Bay-to-Breakers*, Ward Schumaker created a clownish, naked figure of Mercury, painted blue and sporting a red nose (p. 72). Schumaker also developed a number of variations on this figure for retail sale at Nordstrom (pp. 68-71). Gordon Studer's T-shirt for the 1996 *Bay-to-Breakers* (p. 73) likewise features multi-colored runners, these constructed out of geometric shapes. The figure on Scott Johnson's tee for the Barnabas World Missions Run (p. 74) looks to the geometric streamlining of early 20th-century modern art, specifically Umberto Boccioni's now-iconic sculpture, "Unique Forms of Continuity in Space."

The T-shirts on the following four pages were designed by Ward Schumaker to be sold at the Nordstrom department store in conjunction with the 1995 *San Francisco Examiner* Bay-to-Breakers marathon. Because they were intended for retail sale to tourists, these shirts had to complement the official tee (commisioned by *San Francisco Examiner* Charities and also designed by Schumaker; see p. 72) while having enough appeal to convince non-participants to buy a souvenir of the race. In a shirt for children (p. 68), Schumaker cut the race's traditional symbols, the tortoise and the hare, out of the "B+B" of Bay-to-Breakers. For adults, he was free to exploit the wacky reputation of this particular marathon, famous for its costumed runners. A rubber-nosed Mercury appears with a San Francisco cable car for a body (this page) and is featured wearing a helmet (p.70), making reference to the Mercury figure on the official T-shirt. Mercury's winged foot also makes an appearance (p. 71), about to slip on a banana peel. All artwork, says Schumaker, was done "the old-fashioned way," with rapidograph and hand separations. Schumaker's designs were so successful that extra print runs had to be made to accommodate orders taken during the race.

Design Firm:
Schumaker,
San Francisco, CA
Designer/Illustrator:
Ward Schumaker

Ward Schumaker's design for the official 1995 Bay-to-Breakers T-shirt, commissioned by *San Francisco Examiner* Charities, sponsor of the marathon, appeared on posters as well. The nude blue Mercury with the red-rubber nose salutes the race's many costumed—and uncostumed—participants alike: Schumaker reports that a number of nude, blue-painted runners joined in the 1995 race.

Design Firm:
Schumaker,
San Francisco, CA
Designer/Illustrator:
Ward Schumaker

The bright and colorful runners on Gordon Studer's T-shirt for the 1996 *San Francisco Examiner* Bay-to-Breakers marathon echo the bright and colorful runners who give the race its reputation by appearing in costume. Studer was commissioned by the race's sponsor, *San Francisco Examiner* Charities, to develop a design suitable for printing on a black shirt. Bold geometric shapes in nine colors set the shirt apart from the hand-drawn look of the previous year's T-shirts (see pp. 68-72). Horizontal lines suggest movement and bring to mind the stripes on one of San Francisco's newest monuments, the Museum of Modern Art building by Mario Botta. The design budget was $5500; 72,000 shirts were printed.

SAN FRANCISCO EXAMINER CHARITIES

Design Firm:
Studer Design,
Emeryville, CA
Designer/Illustrator:
Gordon Studer

The Barnabas World Missions Run is not simply a marathon. It is also a fundraiser, held to generate awareness, pledges, and donations to facilitate the organization's missionary work. Administrators of the Barnabas World Missions Run requested from the designer, Scott Johnson, a flexible logo that could be subtly modified, quickly and easily, to suit different destinations and uses worldwide. Johnson, inspired by Umberto Boccioni's streamlined sculpture, "Unique Forms of Continuity in Space," constructed a geometricized Mercury figure who appears to have a great set of "wheels." The image was created in Adobe Illustrator, which allows for the modifications desired by the client. Johnson donated his design services; the printing budget totaled $1500.

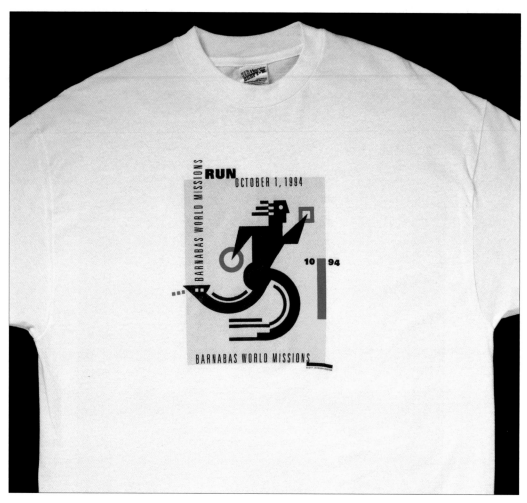

Design Firm:
Scott Johnson Design,
Rockford, IL
Designer/Illustrator:
Scott Johnson

Some of the most attractive T-shirts to be found in this volume of T-shirt promotions relate to religious and charitable events, indicating that the religious community in particular is beginning to grasp the value of design as a means of drawing young people into faith. Of course, T-shirts have long served as souvenirs for charity fundraisers, and the examples shown here range from the simply humorous to the sweetly poignant. Examples of the simply humorous include Dana Willett's bowl of "everything plus the kitchen sink" chili (p. 84), created for the High Country Chilly Chili Challenge (a scholarship benefit), and Robert Neubecker's engaging fishing scenes for two environmental conservation events held by the Eagle Valley Chapter of Trout Unlimited (pp. 82-83). As for poignant, shirts for two events to benefit children and one AIDS walkathon take this approach. Nancy Steinman's tee commemorating Asher/Gould Advertising's participation in the 1995 Los Angeles AIDS Walk (p. 85) refigures an AIDS ribbon as a schematic diagram of the walk's route. The loop in the ribbon implies that movement toward a cure may not always move in forward fashion, but that the route must be traveled nevertheless. Rhodes Stafford Wines Creative's design for a tee given to Texas Instruments participants in and supporters of a Juvenile Diabetes "Walk for the Cure" (pp. 86-87) features a shoelace tied sweetly into the shape of a heart. The children on a shirt by Kerry Allen of SullivanPerkins for a Pamela Blumenthal Children's Mental Health Fund of the Dallas Mental Health Association (p. 88) are the most poignant of all. Though reaching skyward as if in joyful abandon, their ethereal shapes invoke the fragility of childhood.

Compared to the humor and poignancy of the charity T-shirts, the designs for the religious community share a bolder esthetic, as if to announce their arrival on the graphic landscape with the strongest statement possible. Graphica's Ionic column icon (pp. 80-81), on a tee promoting an annual festival hosted by the Annunciation Greek Orthodox Church, literally explodes with celebratory excitement. Habitat for Humanity International, a non-profit, ecumenical Christian housing ministry, recently opened a diversity department. To introduce it, a T-shirt created in-house by the HFHI art department integrates a number of graphic elements, both representational (hands, hammer, houses) and decorative (dots, stripes, dotted lines, zig-zag patterns), to incorporate a theme of "Building Together" (p. 78). Edmon Design's tee for "Triennium" (p. 79), a youth event sponsored by the Christian Church in Kentucky (Disciples of Christ), employs many of the same decorative elements, building with them an abstract figure topped by an eye to suggest an image of God instead of a more realistic (or clichéd) portrayal. In Like Flynn's T-shirt for a conference sponsored by Calvary Chapel of Albuquerque (following spread) is one of the very few shirts in this book to employ photographic imagery. A design composed of four colorized photos evocative of the theme—"Ministering in Grace—Speaking the Truth in Love: A Pastor and Christian Workers Conference"—and a Biblical passage link the shirt to a registration brochure. The photographic and type treatment gives the shirt a contemporary feel not usually associated with the religious community.

Religions and religious organizations have long sought to draw more people into the fold; the 1990s are no exception. Recent years have seen an unexpected and increasingly sophisticated use of the T-shirt as a way to attract people, particularly teenagers, to religion and religious causes. The display of traditional sacred symbolism on T-shirts could be construed as sacrilegious, and would not be likely to serve a proselytistic purpose, in any case. The closest one comes to finding the traditional signifiers of religion on these tees is a Biblical passage used on one shirt (this spread) for its decorative typographic effect as much as its message. This T-shirt, by In Like Flynn for a conference hosted by Calvary Chapel of Albuquerque, shares with Edmon Design's shirt for the Christian Church in Kentucky a contemporary, hip look. The Edmon shirt (p. 79), promoting a religious event for young people, at first glance looks more like an "art garment" than a vehicle for attracting teens to the Christian Church. Graphica's tee for a festival sponsored by the Annunciation Greek Orthodox Church (pp. 80-81) utilizes a decidedly un-Christian motif—the Ionic column—to stress the cultural rather than religious aspect of Greek heritage. A T-shirt for Habitat for Humanity (p. 78), an ecumenical Christian organization that seeks to improve housing for the poor worldwide, emphasizes racial diversity through a harmonious use of color in a design developed in-house.

Design Firm:
In Like Flynn,
Albuquerque, NM
Art Director/Designer:
Dan Flynn
Photographer:
David Nufer
Typography:
Cara Flynn

In 1995, Calvary Chapel of Albuquerque, New Mexico, sponsored "Ministering in Grace—Speaking the Truth in Love: A Pastor and Christian Workers Conference." In Like Flynn created this T-shirt to work in unison with other conference materials, like the brochure shown here. Four images (one stock, the others commissioned) evoke the themes of the conference: lips for speaking, heart for loving, the new King James Version of the Bible for guidance, and a "one way" sign to remind pastors that "The Gospel can easily get lost in a syrupy maze of user-friendliness," as it is stated by the conference host in the brochure. A relevant Bible passage (also printed in the brochure) wraps around the side of the shirt from front to back. Designer Dan Flynn gives credit to his printer for his willingness to tackle a difficult job that required an extra run for the type around the shirt. Puff ink was used for the black type. The shirts were so popular that they were reprinted for sale at the church's bookstore.

CALVARY CHAPEL OF ALBUQUERQUE

Habitat for Humanity International (HFHI) is a non-profit, ecumenical Christian housing ministry that aims to alleviate poverty housing worldwide. Designed by the HFHI art department, this T-shirt introduces a newly established Diversity Department, formed to increase awareness among the general public as to the need for diversity in accomplishing the mission of HFHI, and to attract a more varied group of corporate sponsors, volunteers, and donors. The motif of hands of different races holding a single hammer, surrounded by houses in the same colors to suggest an integrated neighborhood, embodies the central theme of diversity. The design was created in Adobe Illustrator. To ensure that its colors retained their vitality against a black T-shirt, they were printed over white.

Design Firm:
Habitat for Humanity,
Americus, GA
Art Director:
Jerry Counselman
Designer:
Michael Sutton

Design Firm:
Edmon Design,
Lexington, KY
Designer:
Jim Edmon

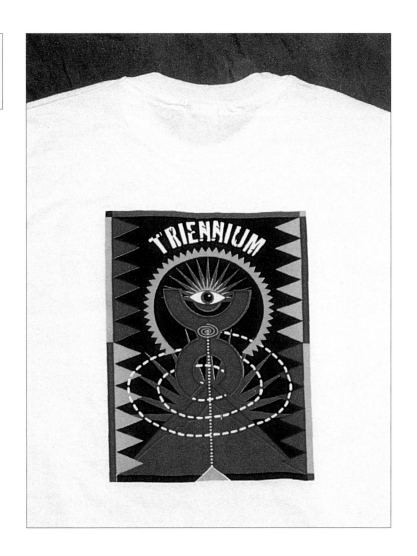

TRIENNIUM
Youth Event
Where's Faith ?
Louisville
Kentucky

ANNUNCIATION GREEK ORTHODOX CHURCH

This celebratory T-shirt promotes an annual festival hosted by the Annunciation Greek Orthodox Church. Graphica's assignment was to develop an icon that emphasizes the historical nature of Greek culture while adding contemporary appeal. Graphica chose an enduring Greek symbol, the Ionic column, and gave it new life. The colored stripes representing the grooves in the column press upward through the capital, where they explode like confetti or fireworks. White underprinting enhances the color printed on a black background.

Design Firm:
Graphica,
Miamisburg, OH
Art Director:
Nick Stamas
Designer:
Geoff Reichel

Promotional materials for charity events usually put a fun face on a serious issue. Save the heart-wrenching testimonials for media coverage, or at least the board of trustees dinner—the charity T-shirt usually needs to appeal to those who want to enjoy themselves while doing good. A shirt by Dana Willett of Advertising Design Systems for the High Country Chilly Chili Challenge (p. 84) makes little reference to the event's beneficiaries (scholarship students), but the promise of chili made of everything including the kitchen sink adds excitement to a quietly important cause. Robert Neubecker's designs for clean-up and fundraising activities to benefit the Eagle Valley Chapter of Trout Unlimited (this spread) use visual humor related to the actual setting—the Eagle River, which runs through this small Colorado mountain town. A tee by Rhodes Stafford Wines Creative for Texas Instruments' participation in a Juvenile Diabetes walk (pp. 86-87) emphasizes the "heart" of those who join in to help, while Asher/Gould's design for the 1995 Los Angeles AIDS Walk employs a new icon expressing concern, the AIDS ribbon, to make its point (p. 85). A SullivanPerkins tee for donors to the Pamela Blumenthal Children's Mental Health Fund in Dallas (p. 88) makes use of playful elements—images of a boy and girl, amusing lettering effects—but the curving and tapered lines of the figural icons add an element of poignancy suited to the gravity of the charitable cause involved.

The Eagle Valley Chapter of Trout Unlimited concerns itself with preserving the environment around the Eagle River, in a small mountain town near Vail, Colorado. Robert Neubecker illustrated these T-shirts for fundraising events pro-bono, at the behest of an active Trout Unlimited member, his brother. Neubecker sought to create simple designs of professional quality that could be reproduced in small quantities through color photocopying. The Fishing Contest tee was developed in one morning, using Photoshop. Both shirts are notable for their humor: a proud dog displaying his catch, an old boot; a fisherman triumphant over his giant foe, a whitefish. (According to Neubecker, fishermen consider whitefish to be "trash" fish, not worth keeping. The event involved catching— and releasing—as many whitefish as possible in one hour.) Both shirts also sport the Trout Unlimited logo on the sleeve or back, and the back of the River Cleanup shirt displays the logos of two sponsors, the Vail Recreation District and Vail Associates, Inc.

Design Firm:
Neubecker Illustration,
Salt Lake City, UT
Designer/Illustrator:
Robert Neubecker

Boone, North Carolina's High Country Chilly Chili Challenge is held every November both to bring some heat to a cold-weather month and to raise funds for scholarships awarded to local high school students. Designer/illustrator Dana Willett of Advertising Design Systems can claim special inspiration for this shirt, produced for the 1995 contest: She was a winning chili-maker in the 1994 event. Cooks compete in a number of categories, including freestyle, where anything goes. Willett's bowl, which includes everything you'd expect *plus* the kitchen sink, makes reference to some of the wild flavors concocted by the participants, such as rattlesnake, crawfish, and kangaroo chili. A chili pepper from the border, surrounded by circles of type giving sponsorship information, serves as a logo for the shirt back.

Design Firm:
Advertising Design
Systems, Boone, NC
Art Director/Designer/
Illustrator:
Dana Willett

AIDS WALK LOS ANGELES '95

START   FINISH

ASHER/GOULD ADVERTISING

With the California Department of Health Services AIDS Awareness as a client, Asher/Gould Advertising thought it important to demonstrate its commitment by participating in an AIDS Walk held in 1995. The motif of the AIDS ribbon is transformed here (with some poetic license) to represent the walk's route. The loop in the ribbon/route also suggests that the path to an AIDS cure may not always move straight ahead, but we must continue to move forward to the finish—a cure. Because the budget for this project was small, the T-shirt was printed in 2-color and the art drawn by the designer, Nancy Steinman.

Design Firm:
Asher/Gould
Advertising,
Los Angeles, CA
Art Director/Designer:
Nancy Steinman
Creative Director:
Bruce Dundore

The Human Resources department of Texas Instruments commissioned Rhodes Stafford Wines Creative to produce a T-shirt for company participants and supporters of a Juvenile Diabetes fundraiser. The sneaker with a heart tied into its laces became an appealing, child-friendly visual icon for the 1995 "Walk for the Cure." The shirt was also entered in a best T-shirt contest held in conjunction with the walk. All art was generated in-house by Rhodes Stafford Wines.

Design Firm:
Rhodes Stafford Wines
Creative, Dallas, TX
Art Director:
Brad Wines
Designer:
Andrew Roth

SullivanPerkins designer Kelly Allen created this T-shirt for a fundraiser to benefit the Pamela Blumenthal Children's Mental Health Fund, part of the Dallas Mental Health Association. By depicting two joyful yet delicate figures, Allen sought to capture the innocence and fragility of childhood and to evoke an emotional response that would encourage additional donations. The T-shirt was given to contributors to the Pamela Blumental Fund to identify them as "Pam's Pals." Allen's type, alternating between white and purple letters, can be read both in typical horizontal fashion and in a playful zig-zag effect.

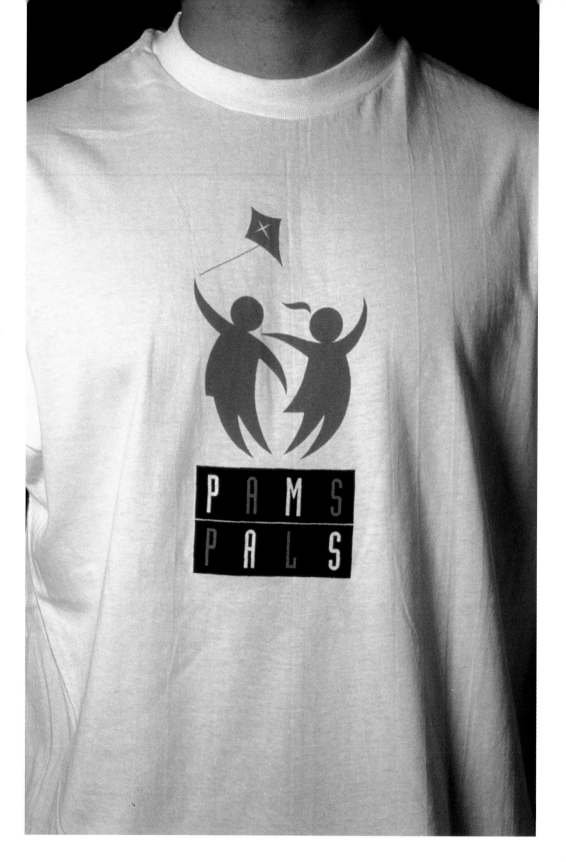

Design Firm:
SullivanPerkins,
Dallas, TX
Art Director/Designer:
Kelly Allen

The T-shirts in this section, which promote markets, museums, and music, employ a variety of visual strategies, from bold, simple graphics to eloquent, poetic art. Two designs announcing urban renewal projects take the bold and simple route to best integrate a number of different objects and images. Witherspoon Advertising's design for Sundance Square (following spread), a revitalized downtown area in Fort Worth, Texas, employs a cut-paper style to depict the many entertainment, shopping, and eating possibilities of the spot: a shopping bag, a guitar, a movie ticket and bag of popcorn, and so on. Sun, moon, and stars also reinforce that Sundance Square offers a wealth of activities from "Sunup To Sundown." The same cut-paper elements, some in different colors, are also used on a billboard. A T-shirt for the groundbreaking ceremonies of River Market, in Little Rock, Arkansas, similarly highlights the objects to be offered for sale, mainly fruits, vegetables, and flowers. Stone & Ward worked from the River Market logo (the initial *M* intertwined with a vine and embellished with fruits and flowers), surrounding it with four blocks containing fresh produce. The objects in the boxes are shadowed with black ink applied in a stipple effect.

Grafik Communication's T-shirt for the National Museum of the American Indian (p. 94) also adapts a previously existing logo to create a new effect. Tribal symbols used on museum stationery were reworked in a smart design that honors Native American heritage. Delro Rosco, too, keeps alive a vanishing tradition with his beautiful illustration for a T-shirt sold at Hawaii's Plantation Village (p. 95). The linear quality of the scratchboard rendering is well-suited to capturing the sugar cane field scene with just the right amount of nostalgia. In contrast, Ted Wright's image of a cowboy hat-wearing, guitar-playing singer for the Country Music Hall of Fame (p. 100) was intended to be anything but nostalgic. Solid blocks of bright color give the shirt a contemporary feel, to attract consumers in the under-40 age group. Wright has also produced a number of T-shirt designs specifically for country music star Dwight Yoakam (pp. 98-99), who takes his image seriously enough to serve as art director on such projects. Wright portrays Yoakam's musical genius—and demonstrates his own (visual) virtuosity—with designs ranging from the enamel-like to the sensitively linear.

Two of the T-shirts in this section represent efforts toward the preservation of vanishing or vanished aspects of American culture, and two promote attempts at its revitalization. Sundance Square, in Fort Worth, Texas, is a rehabilitated downtown, part of a movement away from the malls and back into the heart of a city. Witherspoon Advertising's T-shirt (this spread) conveys the vigor and excitement of the area through brightly-colored symbols. River Market, in Little Rock, Arkansas, also re-establishes the farmer's market tradition that had been lost to our cities. Like the Sundance Square T-shirt, the River Market tee (p. 92), by Stone & Ward, relies on the appeal of fresh, vivid colors to evoke a more vibrant, personal experience than can be found at the supermarket. Hawaii's Plantation Village is a museum that aims to preserve a record of the state's fast-disappearing sugar industry and plantation history. Delro Rosco's 2-color scratchboard illustration captures the scene with an air of nostalgia that might not have been possible with a more realistic visual treatment (p. 95). A T-shirt designed for the Smithsonian's National Museum of the American Indian (p. 94) represents both preservation and revitalization. Grafik Communications' tee employs Native American symbols in a way that respects little-known art forms and celebrates the reopening of a museum that had long languished in a cramped and outdated facility.

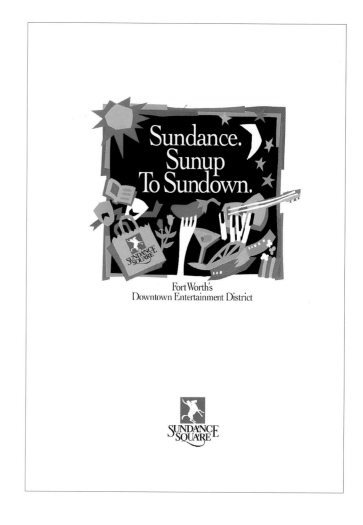

Sundance Square is a revitalized downtown area in Fort Worth, Texas. Witherspoon Advertising was commissioned to provide a festive logo to convey the entertainment, shopping, and eating possibilities available in the area from dawn to dusk. The image had to work on everything from a paper cup to a billboard. A picture suggesting that Sundance Square equals fun was achieved through a sophisticated cut-paper style. The collage incorporates icons ranging from a Tex-Mex chili pepper to piano keys and a Sundance Square shopping bag. The design was created in Quark XPress and Adobe Illustrator; the total budget for design and printing added up to $5000.

SUNDANCE SQUARE, INC.

Design Firm:
Witherspoon
Advertising,
Fort Worth, TX
**Art Director/Designer/
Illustrator:**
Randy Padorr-Black
Creative Director:
Debra Morrow

Design Firm:
Stone & Ward,
Little Rock, AR
Designer:
Bill Gangluff
Creative Director:
Larry Stone

River Market, in Little Rock, Arkansas, houses vendors of fresh flowers, produce, and specialty foods. In designing a T-shirt for attendees of the market's groundbreaking, Stone & Ward surrounded a market logo with images of the basic items for sale: flowers, fruits, and vegetables. Original black-and-white artwork was converted to color using the River Market palette. An invitation to the groundbreaking event took unique form, packaged in a flowerpot, to emphasize the concept of planting a new market within the city and to evoke the freshness of the items that would eventually be offered to the public.

RIVER MARKET

When the Smithsonian Institution's National Museum of the American Indian moved to new quarters in downtown Manhattan, Grafik Communications was brought in to design a T-shirt for retail sale. The museum wanted something that was fashionable yet reflective of its mission and the diversity of Native American culture, at an affordable price for the general public. The Grafik Communications design team produced this image, drawing on tribal symbols and colors that had been adapted as part of the museum's identity. Through the use of three different Native American art-based icons, the rich heritage of our country's indigenous peoples is evoked without being trite.

Design Firm:
Grafik Communications, Ltd., Alexandria, VA
Designers:
Melanie Bass,
Julie Sebastianelli,
Judy Kirpich
Illustrator:
Linley Logan
Project Director:
Terence Winch

Hawaii's sugar industry is disappearing in the late 20th century. Plantation Village honors the state's sugar and plantation histories and pays tribute to the many ethnicities that have contributed to Hawaii's diversity. Delro Rosco of Ewa Beach, Hawaii, sought to elicit an emotional response through his illustration, especially from those visitors to the museum who had grown up on or had ties with sugar plantations. Archival photographs provided reference material for Rosco's final scratchboard rendering. The fine-art style of the illustration achieves sophistication within a limited budget. Lettering was done by hand to match the image in style. The front of the shirt features a small detail of the building and smokestack. A custom-mixed cream color was printed over white ink on shirts of various colors. Printing costs were approximately $5 per shirt.

Design Firm:
Delro Rosco Illustration,
Ewa Beach, HI
**Art Director/Designer/
Illustrator:**
Delro Rosco

T-shirts and music seem naturally to go together, like blues and jazz or country and western. The shirts featured here, promoting performers and performances, take as their central image the musician. Muller & Company's tee for the 1995 Kansas City Blues and Jazz Festival (this spread) depicts a saxophone player, eyes closed in concentration, to express the joy music brings to performer and listener alike. Ted Wright's portraits of country music star Dwight Yoakam reflect both the illustrator's respect for the musician and his ability to work in two distinct visual styles. Whether employing a lyrical, decorative mode (p. 98) or depicting Yoakam in bold, block-print fashion, Wright has succeeded in pleasing two tough audiences: country music fans, and the musician himself, who takes his visual appearance very seriously. Wright was the obvious choice to create a T-shirt for the Country Music Hall of Fame, and his design (p. 100) partakes of the same esthetic as the brightly-colored version of Yoakam (p.99), to appeal to younger buyers.

Design Firm:
Muller & Company,
Kansas City, MO
**Art Director/Designer/
Illustrator:**
Jon Simonsen

After creating a poster for the 1995 Kansas City Blues and Jazz Festival, Muller & Company was asked to donate the design for a T-shirt that would complement the poster and "sell a ton." The main elements of the poster—the musician's head, the mouthpiece of his saxophone, and the lettering —were reworked as a logo and simplified in order to make the painterly image more suited to silkscreening. The logo, in blues-evoking shades of blue, was then used on cups and hats as well as tees. On the back of the shirt, the figure is printed in negative in red, surrounded by additional information about each day's programs and the musicians involved. Because the annual festival is completely not-for-profit, employees of Muller & Company also employed their "wonderful begging skills" in securing donated services for the entire T-shirt production.

KANSAS CITY BLUES AND JAZZ FESTIVAL

Illustrator Ted Wright describes his assignment for the black-and-white shirt displayed on this page: "To create a hip, one-color, honky tonk'n T-shirt for Hollywood's hillbilly song-writer and singer . . . Dwight Yoakam." Wright character-izes the country music star as "a perfectionist," "very articulate when it comes to art," and "very aware of what he wants to portray in his promotional images. Dwight is truly a musical visionary and the images in his music and videos exude his personal artistic direction." In fact, Yoakam served as the art director for the shirt on this page, created for Boreman Entertainment in Los Angeles. The design was drawn in black ink, with color separations done in Adobe Illustrator. For the 6-color images of Yoakam (opposite page), Wright sought to portray the singer as a white-hatted good guy and an icon of country style and fashion. Working from photographs, he created an immediately recognizable portrait of the artist.

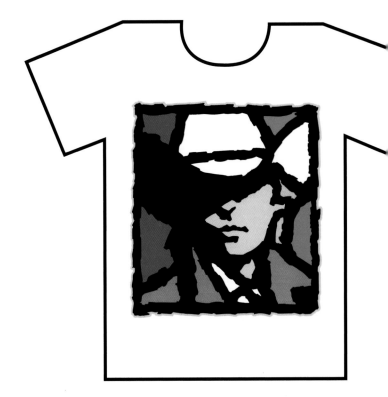

Design Firm:
Honky Tonk West,
Hillsboro, MO
Art Director:
Dwight Yoakam
Designer/Illustrator:
Ted Wright

COUNTRY MUSIC HALL OF FAME

The Country Music Hall of Fame in Nashville, Tennessee, hired Ted Wright to design an exciting graphic depicting a country singer or performance, to be used on a shirt sold to younger music fans at the museum. The image needed to be large and contemporary to appeal to the under-40 age bracket. Wright utilized vibrant colors and bold shapes for immediate visual impact. The result is a tee that stands above the average Nashville tourist shirt and proved very popular with young people. Wright reports that he worked from his own photographs of various singers and performers, and the figure portrayed in his design bears more than a passing resemblance to country music star Dwight Yoakam (see previous spread). Color separations were done in Adobe Illustrator and the shirt printed in 8-color. The image was also used on costume jewelry.

Design Firm:
Country Music
Hall of Fame,
Nashville, TN
Art Director:
Brooke Kingston
Designer/Illustrator:
Ted Wright

Of the T-shirts featured in this section, which promote brands, stores, and products, or are offered for retail sale on the basis of good-looking design, many seem intended to appeal to four groups of people: those who enjoy nature and the outdoors, beverage drinkers, art lovers, and those who are still kids at heart. Though Brazos Sportwear's T-shirts for Mickey & Co. (following spread) are aimed at a youth market, who can resist the world's favorite mouse? Shirts for BRIO Corporation, by The Design Foundry (p. 114) and James & Bragstad Design (p. 115) are meant to sell toys to kids, but no doubt many parents find the gardening tools and wooden railway toys irresistible. Dino's Kachino's (p. 104), amusing figures that populate an imaginary tribe of "Italian Indians," are fun for child and adult alike.

While the fancifully-decorated animals by Kristen Balouch of Zubi Design for tees sold by Kabuko Inc. suggest child's play, the "endangered" label and Balouch's subtle environmental commentary make them attractive to anyone concerned with the natural world (pp. 130-133). Beautiful scratchboard illustrations by Peter Byer on the theme of "The Nature of Sport," offered for sale on T-shirts by Coming Attractions (pp. 106-108), appeal to serious outdoor enthusiasts, such as hikers, climbers, and canoeists. Outdoor enthusiasts of another sort—boisterous mountain bikers—are targeted with J.J. Sedelmaier Productions' "Psychotraining" T-shirt (pp. 110-111), for Converse. Those who enjoy fishing (or just looking at fish) will appreciate the earthy coloration of Alison Linksy's "Two Fish" (p. 128), for Marianne's Screenprinting, and the wacky humor of 2nd Globe's "The One That Should Have Gotten Away" (p. 136).

The buff and bare-chested dude chugging a bottle of Ocean Spray juice on a shirt by Devine & Pearson Advertising (p. 113) suggests a person who craves the active life—how else would he have developed those pecs? Those whose preferred concept of the active life revolves around the social rather than the natural sphere will appreciate a T-shirt and a tie depicting elegantly clad figures lifting glasses of the aperitif Dubonnet (p. 112), by Halbleib/Beggs Advertising for Heaven Hill Distilleries. Those whose idea of the active life requires caffeine will love a series of shirts by Gotham City Graphics that celebrate the joys of coffee (pp. 118-122).

Finally, a number of shirts shown here appeal to art lovers of all kinds. Christina Neill's delicate woodcuts of plants and flowers, for three shirts by Marianne's Screenprinting (pp. 123-125), bring fine art to the world of tees, as do Christopher Mayes's "Sunflowers" (p. 127) and "America" (p. 126), sold through his own T-shirt company, Hold the Mayo. Alison Linsky's "Arty-choke" (p. 135), for Marianne's Screenprinting, adds a bit of humor to a natural theme, while Scott Peek's "Skelly" (pp. 116-117), for Standard Deluxe, brings humor to a supernatural theme. And for those who enjoy making art of their own, Maxine Boll-Hughes's T-shirt for The Tomato Factory, a knitting supplies shop, helps to raise the craft of knitting to the level of art (p.109).

Most of the designers assigned to promote particular stores, brands, and products through the T-shirts displayed in this section have relied upon the depiction of characters and figures. Mickey Mouse, of course, needs no introduction, but how can a designer present him in a fresh way? Brazos Sportswear approaches this problem with the idea of creating newly "classic" designs for a classic character, such as "Big Circle Mickey" and "Full Flower Mickey" (this spread). J.J. Sedelmaier Productions developed a thrill-seeking mountain biker for a series of "Psychotraining" commercials for Converse. The psycho-biker proved so popular that he now appears on a Converse tee (pp. 110-111). Inspired by Hopi kachina dolls, Dino Paul of Dino Design has invented an entire cast of characters, Dino's Kachino's (pp. 104-105). A Devine & Pearson Advertising T-shirt for Ocean Spray depicts a powerful, superhero-type character chugging a single-serve juice drink (p. 113). Not only is this guy cool, but his impressive physique suggests that Ocean Spray beverages played a part in attaining it. The characters shown on a Dubonnet T-shirt and tie by Halbleib/Beggs may be more human, but they, too, are cool—and chic (p. 112). The figures in Coming Attractions' "Nature of Sport" tees (pp. 106-108), originally produced for outdoor sporting goods retailer Eastern Mountain Sports, are so in tune with the environment that their reflections take the

shape of animals. Designs for BRIO Corporation T-shirts, by The Design Foundry (p. 114) and James & Bragstad Design (p. 115), feature the company's toys in an appealing, artistic manner, and a shirt for the yarn and knitting store The Tomato Factory (p. 109), by Maxine Boll-Hughes, eschews overt reference to people and products in favor of an almost Pop Art pattern evocative of the store's modern view of knitting.

Brazos Sportswear (formerly Velva Sheen/Genus Manufacturing Company) is a licensed manufacturer and vendor of Disney apparel under the Mickey & Co. brand name. Vice president of merchandising and design Janet Reuter explains that Brazos seeks to integrate the Mickey Mouse character into classic new designs, more "upscale" than had been seen in the past. In the Brazos production process, Reuter provides market research–based design direction to the art director, who revises and fine-tunes the art. For one shirt (opposite page), a horizontally striped background was selected to complement the circular forms around which Mickey is built. The "Full Flower Mickey" (this page) was created with the aim of developing a fresh style for the character in the juniors apparel market. To duplicate the look and feel of real flowers, dozens of flower photos were scanned, with shadows added for depth. The resulting pattern was cut into a recognizable Mickey shape. Plastisol inks were printed in 4-color stochastic process.

THE WALT DISNEY CO.

Design Firm:
Brazos Sportswear, Cincinnati, OH
Art Director:
Bob Powers
V.P. Merchandising & Design:
Janet Reuter
Illustrators:
Lance Lee, Rob Zumstein

DINO'S KACHINO'S

Dino Paul uses T-shirts as the vehicle for bringing to life a fictitious Indian tribe, Dino's Kachino's. According to Paul, many years ago a small Native American tribe journeyed to Rimini, Italy, where they recreated cliffside dwellings similar to those at home, and embraced "deeply embedded Italian spiritual beliefs," such as "spaghetti westerns, soft loafers, and dramatic fashion standards." To celebrate this new life, the tribe "anointed a young brave named Dino to create symbolic icons that would serve as blessings of adventure, joy and willingness"—and as a Dino Design merchandising venture, too. Taking off from Hopi kachina dolls, which are delightfully decorative to non-Hopi eyes, Paul developed 18 characters, each with an individual story told on a hangtag. These characters were drawn directly in Adobe Illustrator, then sent straight to screen through a Screen Jet system. The shirts are printed in 5-color over white underprinting. Each color is pulled twice, with a flash between each color.

Hundreds, maybe thousands, of years ago, a small band of audacious Indians set out from what is now America, and journeyed to a small Italian coastal community on the outskirts of Rimini. The tribe brought with them limber minds and large souls capable of savoring the cultural cornucopia they experienced in transit.

When they finally reached their village, they were dizzy with delight of discovering cliffs along the Adriatic Sea that provided homesites similar to their mountain coves back in North America; and they were eager to embrace the deeply embedded Italian spiritual beliefs – namely, that a life without spaghetti westerns, soft loafers and dramatic fashion standards, is a life without value.

To celebrate their new cliff condos and amalgam of philosophies, the happy tribe adopted an Italian name, Pizio (a shortened version of precipizio d'abitazione – cliff dwellers). They also anointed a young brave named Dino to create symbolic icons that would serve as blessings of adventure, joy and willingness. The icons, through the generations, have come to be known as Dino's Kachinos.

Due to the fact that the Pizio's own no land and have no taste for gambling, they are now offering their beloved ancient designs on clothing and in the form of various products, for a price.

The Pizio's thank you for joining them in the appreciation of uncommon ethnic fusion. May a Dino's Kachino bring you an odd and wonderful day.

Dino's Kachinos ®

The Pizio's are an ecologically conscious people and all of their printed materials utilize recycled papers and the most environmentally safe printing process available.

Design Firm:
Dino Design,
Phoenix, AZ
Art Director/Illustrator:
Dino Paul

Coming Attractions is an imprinted sportswear manufacturer with roots in the outdoor market. The Manassas, Virginia, company originally produced these three T-shirts for customization by Eastern Mountain Sports, an outdoor sporting goods retail chain. To appeal to a customer aged 25 and up, images depicting the "Paddler by Nature," "Hiker by Nature," and "Climber by Nature" were developed, and grouped under a more general theme of "The Nature of Sport." Animals appear as reflections or echoes of the human figures, linking these outdoor enthusiasts with their environment; the rough scratchboard illustrations in blues, browns, and greens further the shirts' eco-friendly appearance. The art was created and colorized by the designer, Peter Byer. Type was kept simple and understated, which also facilitates namedrops: Only one screen need be changed for customization. Design production involved Photoshop and FreeHand; the shirts were printed in 6-color. Now that these designs have passed through their Eastern Mountain Sports production cycle, they are offered for sale as part of Coming Attractions' preprint line.

HIKER BY NATURE

Design Firm
Coming Attractions,
Manassas, VA
Art Director:
Phil Nicholson
Designer/Illustrator:
Peter Byer

Design Firm:
Maxine Boll-Hughes,
Frenchtown, NJ
Art Director/Illustrator:
Maxine Boll-Hughes

The Tomato Factory is a retailer of quality yarns, finished goods, knitting patterns and accessories, and related items. Because the store emphasizes modern, colorful patterns and playful creativity, Maxine Boll-Hughes sought to capture a fresh feel in this T-shirt without being too literal about the products offered. She created the Tomato Factory logo, and feeling that the design was very strong, decided to repeat it in nine colors for the T-shirt, which was available to store customers and at a trade show. The ultimate effect goes beyond an old-fashioned conception of knitting to one that suggests modern art, *à la* Andy Warhol.

THE TOMATO FACTORY

After producing a number of successful "Psychotraining" commercials for sporting goods manufacturer Converse, J.J. Sedelmaier Productions was commissioned to follow up with T-shirts employing the same character, a stereotypically danger-loving, anything-goes mountain biker. On-staff artist Gideon Kendall developed the arresting image of the psycho-biker, loosely rendered in a woodcut-like style that also suggests the dirt and mud of the mountain biking experience. The front and back of the shirt tell a story—the biker comes at you on the front, depicted in extreme perspective. The tread of the bike wheel is echoed by the tread on the bottom of the biker's Converse shoes, which are emphasized with blue ink. On the tee's back, the biker leaves you "in the dust" as he (or she) rides away, the Converse logo his/her Zorro-like signature. The shirt was screenprinted in 8-color with Plastisol inks.

Design Firm:
J.J. Sedelmaier
Productions, Inc.,
White Plains, NY
Art Director:
J.J. Sedelmaier
Designers:
J.J. Sedelmaier,
Gideon Kendall
Illustrator:
Gideon Kendall

Halbleib/Beggs Advertising positioned the aperitif Dubonnet (a Heaven Hill Distilleries brand) with catchphrases like "When cocktails won't dū" and "Dūit any time." Burton Morris's lively illustrations of chic Dubonnet imbibers were selected to set the brand apart from the proliferation of slice-of-life photography in the distilled spirits industry. This T-shirt and tie, to be used in off- and on-premise promotions, continue the high-keyed color and stylized look now identified with the Dubonnet brand. While translating a 4-color print campaign into a multicolor screenprint for the T-shirt was relatively simple, the tie design required adapting the imagery into a running pattern by arranging illustrative elements into a random continuing pattern. The T-shirt was printed in 6-color. The tie, in 7-color on silk, was produced in Italy.

Design Firm:
Halbleib/Beggs
Advertising, Louisville, KY
Art Director/Designer:
Mary H. Reilly
Illustrator:
Burton Morris
Copywriter:
Bob Beggs
Creative Director:
Steve Kuhlman

Ocean Spray looked to Devine & Pearson Advertising for a cool T-shirt that would capture the "refreshing, gulpable attitude" of the beverage company's single-serve juice drinks. The tee was intended for use as a trade incentive and consumer promotion. The blocky, superhero-ish illustration was created in-house at Devine & Pearson by designer Greg Wood. Gradations were produced in Adobe Illustrator and the shirts were printed in six spot colors rather than 4-color process in order to best reproduce the gradations and to keep the colors vibrant. The design and illustration budget totaled $4650.

OCEAN SPRAY

Design Firm:
Devine & Pearson
Advertising, Quincy, MA
Designer/Illustrator:
Greg Wood

The T-shirts featured in this spread were created by two Wisconsin firms, The Design Foundry and James & Bragstad Design, for BRIO Corporation, manufacturers of high-end children's toys. The garden tools shirt on this page, by The Design Foundry, is meant to be worn by retail staff to communicate that playing with BRIO garden tools is fun. Bright fields of solid color surrounded by bold outlines are embellished by flowing lines of type to maintain the impression of BRIO quality while adding a slightly feminine flair requested by the toy company. The design was created in Adobe Illustrator and the shirt printed in 6-color process using water-based inks. James & Bragstad's images for BRIO (opposite page) were developed to promote the company's "Wooden Railway Engineer's Club." The design, done in Adobe Illustrator, needed to be flexible for adaptation to future projects such as brochures and newsletters. James & Bragstad's use of primary colors and simple, clean drawings of the engine and caboose (front and back, of course) helped to keep the project "problem-free," according to the firm. Due to cost restrictions, gray tones were created using different screens on black. The color used for the wheel caps was the only actual gray ink employed for printing.

Design Firm:
The Design Foundry, Madison, WI
Art Directors/Designers:
Jane Jenkins, Tom Jenkins

Design Firm:
James & Bragstad Design,
Milwaukee, WI
Art Director/Designer:
Elizabeth James
Computer Illustration:
Nina Schrage

The "art garments" in this section, T-shirts for retail sale mainly on the strength of their imagery, fall loosely into three categories: art for art's sake; art for fun's sake; and art for animals' sake. Christiana Neill's delicate woodcuts of geraniums, ivy, and paper whites for tees by Marianne's Screenprinting (pp. 123-125) bring an original art touch to an often blatantly commercial medium. Christopher Mayes's "Sunflowers" and "America" T-shirts (pp. 126-127) also look to fine art—in this case, Pop Art—for some of their appeal. Another shirt for Marianne's Screenprinting, "Two Fish" (pp. 128-129), illustrated by Alison Linksy, employs a Pop Art repeat as well, while her "Arty-choke" (pp. 134-135) puns on artistic pretensions. The fish motif appears again on 2nd Globe's "The One That Should Have Gotten Away" (p. 136), a visual pun that takes the form of a fish-eats-man tale. "Skelly" (this spread) remains as fresh and fun as the moment he first appeared as a doodle on the sketchpad of Standard Deluxe's Scott Peek. Gotham City Graphic's coffee series (pp. 118-122) both celebrates and satirizes the caffeine-addicted among us. And finally, Kristen Balouch utilizes the charm of highly decorated animals such as an elephant with dotted legs and a striped trunk to bring attention to endangered species in a line of shirts for Kabuko Inc. (pp. 130-133): art for animals' sake.

Design Firm:
Standard Deluxe, Inc.,
Waverly, AL
Designer/Illustrator:
Scott Peek

Standard Deluxe is a design and silkscreen printshop with a product line of wholesale preprinted designs by various artists. This image was created in-house by designer/illustrator Scott Peek. "Skelly" originated as a sketchbook doodle, and the final design was barely manipulated in order to maintain its freshness. The doodle was enlarged on a copy camera directly to film positive. The snake and logo were placed on a second acetate for a simple 2-color separation, and the image was handprinted on Standard Deluxe's largest palette for T-shirts: 16 1/2" tall. Because the project was done in-house, "for fun," there was "no real budget."

STANDARD DELUXE

Gotham City Graphics describes the audience for this line of T-shirts as enthusiasts of coffee and coffee imagery, outer space, and science. The firm's mail-order T-shirt business serves as an outlet for the designers' playful, whimsical style, and in this case, their passion for coffee. The entire series exploits a retro appeal, in both slick and gritty forms, and the computer had only a minor role in the production process. Two-color printing on white means that the shirts remain affordable. "Industrial Strength Coffee" (this page) derives impact from a hazardous warning shade of orange; "Hot Delicious Coffee" (opposite page) shares the welcoming feel of an old-fashioned diner; "Planet Coffee" (p. 120) evokes a fifties sci-fi comic book; "Scientific Brain Treatment" (p. 121) displays the molecular structure of caffeine; and the positive/negative "Day or Night Coffee is Just Right" (p. 122) looks like an old matchbook, with a rough feel achieved through many generations of photocopies and a mocha color.

Design Firm:
Gotham City Graphics,
Burlington, VT
Art Director/Illustrator:
Stephanie Salmon
Designers:
Amey Radcliffe,
Stephanie Salmon

With the three T-shirts shown on the following pages, Marianne's Screenprinting attempted to break away from the computer art now seen in many designs. Christiana Neill created three lovely woodcuts, "Geranium" (this page), "Ivy" (p. 124), and "Paper Whites" (p. 125), which provide attractive images well suited to 1-color screenprinting on T-shirts in a variety of colors. The woodcuts were scanned into Photoshop and then into Corel 5 for Windows 3.1 in order to size and output the film for screen work. The high-tech computer production results in shirts of unusual fine-art appeal. The series was offered wholesale to retailers in the spring of 1996.

MARIANNE'S SCREENPRINTING

Design Firm:
Marianne's
Screenprinting, Inc.,
Vineyard Haven, MA
Designer:
Christiana Neill

For these two T-shirt designs, Christopher Mayes takes two familiar artistic icons, the American flag and the sunflower, and gives them a personal twist. Mayes's signature device, the multiple step and repeat, makes reference to Andy Warhol's borrowing of the silkscreen repeat for high-art purposes. Printed in bright colors, both shirts benefit from the strong visual patterns that result. Quirky type treatments provide additional excitement. The shirts, printed in 8-color, were sold in department stores in the spring of 1996.

Design Firm:
Christopher Mayes
Design, Houston, TX
Designer/Illustrator:
Christopher Mayes

This "Two Fish" T-shirt was produced by Marianne's Screenprinting of Vineyard Haven, Massachusetts, an island town, for a spring 1996 wholesale line offered to local resorts and retail stores. Designer/illustrator Alison Linsky's art was meant to appeal to a wide range of customers with its charming design and contemporary color palette. The original art was created in Corel 5 for Windows 3.1.

Design Firm:
Marianne's
Screenprinting, Inc.,
Vineyard Haven, MA
Designer:
Alison Linsky

Designer/illustrator Kristen Balouch of Zubi Design created these T-shirt images for Kabuko Inc., a company in the exclusive gift market industry. For a large audience concerned with environmental issues, Balouch developed broadly graphic designs with subtly conceived messages on the theme of endangered species. The rhinoceros on a pedestal (this page) alludes to the solitude of his future as the last of his kind. A line of Galapagos tortoises (opposite page) is cropped so to suggest a procession into extinction. Elephants (p. 133) wear different expressions on their faces—sadness, anger, fear—to symbolize reactions to the possible loss of species. Balouch drew the images in FreeHand, creating fanciful imagined animals in attractive high-key colors and animated patterns, perhaps suggesting that, without protection, these endangered animals might one day exist in our imaginations only.

FIJI BANDED IGUANA

ENDANGERED

Design Firm:
Zubi Design,
Brooklyn, NY
Art Director/Illustrator:
Kristen Balouch

"Arty-choke" was created by Alison Linsky as part of Marianne's Screenprinting's spring 1996 wholesale T-shirt line, sold to area retailers. The punning design was developed to take advantage of currently popular colors and to complement a new shade of shirt, "putty," as well as traditional white. The original illustration was scanned into Corel 5 for Windows 3.1, where it was manipulated for color and effect.

Design Firm:
Marianne's
Screenprinting, Inc.,
Vineyard Haven, MA
Designer/Illustrator:
Alison Linsky

Chris Beatty and David Jemerson Young collaborated on the design for this shirt, "The One That Should Have Gotten Away," for their company, 2nd Globe, purveyors of art garments. Beatty and Young describe the main design problem of this shirt as creating "something with artistic integrity that would also appeal to the wide target audience," comprising fishermen and outdoor recreation enthusiasts. The solution to the problem, fish-eats-man, turned out to be something of a problem—how to overprint the shirt's collar with two inks. Young drew the design in pen and ink, then Beatty worked the drawing onto the garment and created a second color template behind the cross-hatched design. After some convincing, the pressman agreed to print the tricky collar.

Design Firm:
2nd Globe,
Indianapolis, IN
Art Director/
Creative Director:
Chris Beatty
Illustrator:
David Jemerson Young